Literacy Play Centers

by

Maureen Walcavich

and

Karen Bauer

Carson-Dellosa Publishing Company, Inc.
Greensboro, North Carolina

 Credits

Editor: Joey Bland

Layout Design: Van Harris

Inside Illustrations: Janet Armbrust and Van Harris

Cover Design: Matthew Van Zomeren

Cover Illustrations: Matthew Van Zomeren

ISBN 978-1-59441-784-9

Table of Contents

Introduction...4
Overview...6
   The Importance of Play in Children's Development................................6
   What Are Literacy Play Centers?..7
   The Value of Literacy Play Centers...7
   Planning and Preparation..10
   Preparing Children..14
Implementing Literacy Play Centers...15
   Introducing the Centers..15
   Procedures While the Center Is Open..16
   Activities to Build Letter Recognition...16
   Activities to Build Mathematical Skills and Concepts............................19
   Coordinating with Other Existing Classroom Centers............................20
   Documenting Children's Learning 20
   Closing the Literacy Play Centers...20
Literacy Play Centers Chart..22
Letters/Sounds Index...27
Math Skills Index..29
The Literacy Play Centers
   Grocery Store...31
   Pizza Restaurant..38
   Fast-Food Restaurant...44
   Doctor's Office..51
   Shoe Store...58
   Veterinary Office...65
   Barbershop/Hair Salon..71
   Post Office...77
   Florist Shop...84
   Sporting Goods Store..92
   Home Improvement Store...100
   Bank...107
   Bakery..113
   Optometrist's Office...119
   Movie Theater...127
Assessment of Children's Skills...133
Frequency of Assessing Skills...134
Reproducibles...135
References..156

Introduction

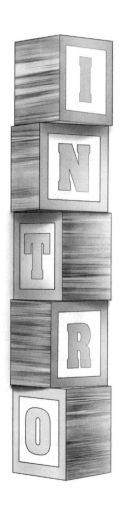

Is it possible for early childhood teachers to provide young children with opportunities to play and still meet standards? The answer is a resounding "Yes!" Teachers in early childhood programs can incorporate play into the curriculum and still meet Head Start Outcomes and state standards for early learning.

Teachers of young children know that children learn through active involvement. Integrated thematic units and in-depth projects are appropriate approaches for teaching young children. Early childhood teachers understand that play is one of the ways young children learn about the world. Play actively involves children in consolidating their understanding of experiences, and can be an integral component of integrated thematic units and projects.

This book provides early childhood teachers with 15 literacy play centers that can be incorporated into thematic units of study appropriate for young children. The topics of study can lay the foundation for the curriculum for an entire school year. The experiences provided in each literacy play center build on children's emerging understanding of literacy, mathematics, and their community.

Children develop phonemic awareness in meaningful contexts while they are involved in the literacy play centers. They are introduced to the letters of the alphabet, letter sounds, rhyming words, and syllables as they learn about a variety of businesses in the community. Children also develop book-handling skills and concepts of print as they engage in meaningful reading and writing activities.

Number and shape recognition, classification, one-to-one correspondence, graph creation and interpretation, and counting are also incorporated into the literacy play centers. Young children use money, seriate (arrange) materials by common attributes, and are involved in estimation.

Students develop an understanding of grocery stores, shoe stores, post offices, doctors' offices, and other community businesses as they role-play using real and pretend props in the literacy play centers. Social skills of cooperation, negotiation, and sharing emerge while children play and interact in the various centers.

Each literacy play center is designed to be used independently and includes goals and objectives, in addition to detailed procedures for implementation. There are also lists of props and suggested print and writing materials needed for the centers. Each literacy play center includes a list of children's literature appropriate to that center, as well as suggestions for storing the props and literacy materials.

The literacy play centers are presented in a sequence that can be implemented beginning in September. The first center is Grocery Store since most children have had previous experiences shopping for groceries. The centers progress from places children are most familiar with to those where they may have limited experiences. A Literacy Play Center Chart (see page 22) provides a sequence for implementing the centers, as well as the skills developed and the assessments used in each center.

Each literacy play center builds on knowledge and skills addressed in previous centers. The knowledge and skills are sequenced based on children's emerging literacy and their developing understanding of mathematical concepts and knowledge of the community. The sequence of literacy skills is shown in an index that indicates where letters, sounds, and words are introduced and reinforced. A second index shows the specific math skills addressed in each center.

The final section of the book explains the importance of embedding assessment into the curriculum. A variety of developmentally appropriate assessment instruments are provided. These instruments can be used by the teacher to assess and monitor children's literacy progress throughout the year. Based on the assessment results, teachers can adapt the curriculum to meet the individual needs of children.

Teachers have found literacy play centers to be highly effective in supporting children's emergent literacy, math concepts, and social skills. Play **is** the way young children learn.

     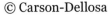

Overview

The Importance of Play in Children's Development

Children are active learners. They construct their understanding of the world through the experiences and interactions they have with people and the environment. As an infant manipulates a mobile hung over his crib, he discovers that objects move when touched. He hits the mobile with varying degrees of force and notices that the objects move differently based on the force used. An infant who smiles at a caregiver is rewarded with a smile from the caregiver. A toddler stacking blocks finds that the blocks sometimes topple over. An adult may stack blocks with the child to provide a model for the toddler to observe. She learns through repeated experiences and interactions how to stack the blocks to prevent them from falling down. Preschoolers manipulate puzzle pieces until they succeed in reconstructing the puzzle. Sometimes, the preschooler is assisted by a parent or caregiver who points out the shapes or colors of puzzle pieces, thus providing cues for the child to use in completing the puzzle. Through these interactions and explorations, children consolidate their knowledge.

Children enjoy playing and are intrinsically motivated to play. Children engaged in play are actively involved. Play is the primary way young children explore the world, and it supports every aspect of development and learning. Levy (1978) said that the most significant attribute of play may be that it unifies the mind, body, and spirit. Early educators, such as Rousseau, Pestalozzi, and Froebel stressed the importance of play in childhood. They saw play as a means for children to learn (Frost, 1992). Contemporary theorists, such as Piaget and Vygotsky, stress the role of play in children's cognitive and social-emotional development.

Recent brain research indicates that the opportunities children are afforded during early childhood are critical to the development of neural pathways that govern cognitive, motor, and socio-emotional learning and development (Shore, 1997). Play is a critical element in early brain development because it provides the context for experiences that are vital to the development of neural pathways (Kieff and Casbergue, 1999). These neural pathways provide the foundation for later academic tasks.

Incorporating play experiences into early education has long been recognized as developmentally appropriate. Play supports children's learning and is vital to their development.

What Are Literacy Play Centers?

Dramatic play naturally emerges around the age of two (Berk, 2005). Preschool children spend much of their time engaged in dramatic play. Programs for preschoolers must provide large blocks of time for children to engage in dramatic play. Children need a minimum of half an hour to become deeply absorbed in their play.

Dramatic play centers, such as Housekeeping, are found in most child care and preschool settings. Including dramatic play centers as integral components of thematic units of study helps children construct their knowledge of the topic being studied through role-playing and active participation in the centers. The dramatic play themes afforded by such centers support children's physical, cognitive, and social-emotional development.

Early childhood programs that add literacy elements to dramatic play centers can enhance emergent literacy. Literacy experiences in dramatic play centers build on children's emerging understanding of oral and written language. We define such dramatic play centers, rich in literacy elements, as literacy play centers. These developmentally appropriate centers offer children play experiences that support their emergent literacy.

The Value of Literacy Play Centers

Teachers at all levels are being held accountable for children's learning. Literacy play centers help lay the foundation for later academic success in school. While involved in literacy play centers, children build on their emerging understanding of the world. Language, emergent literacy, mathematical skills, and social studies concepts can be developed as children play. Through careful development and implementation of literacy play centers, teachers can meet the Head Start Outcomes and early learning standards identified by various states.

One of a child's first steps toward literacy is the development of language (Morrow, 2001). Continuous advancements in oral language development are necessary for literacy growth and development (Antonacci and O'Callaghan, 2005). Literacy play centers promote the development of language because language is learned best when it is embedded within experiences that are meaningful for children (Morrow, 2001). Each literacy play center offers children specific language experiences that expand their vocabulary and their ability to understand and be understood by others.

Vocabulary develops as children are engaged in speaking, listening, reading, and writing. Literacy play centers offer children opportunities to engage in all of these processes. Children will learn words associated with various places located in their communities. For example, as they play in the Pizza Restaurant,

     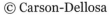

children will learn the meaning of **dough**, **chef**, **delivery**, and **menu**. They will engage in writing orders, reading meaningful print, and listening to children's literature. While playing in the Florist Shop, children will create flower arrangements, make deliveries, and learn the names of different flowers and plants. They will write orders; read charts, signs, and environmental print; and examine catalogs. Similar experiences occur in all of the centers.

Oral communication skills develop as children interact with each other and the teacher in literacy play centers. Children's ability to understand and be understood by others will develop as they engage in conversations and assume the roles of employees and customers in the various centers.

Emergent literacy is enhanced as children interact with environmental print. Environmental print offers children opportunities to understand their world and the ways in which adults use literacy in meaningful contexts (Bauer, Walcavich, and Nipps, 2006). The use of environmental print in each of the literacy centers makes reading meaningful. Children exposed to environmental print construct an understanding of its meaning, and this understanding will expand as children see and recognize environmental print outside of their classrooms.

Children develop concepts of print by handling literacy materials, interpreting the charts and labels in the literacy play centers, and listening to quality literature read as part of the theme study. Concepts of print include an understanding that print, not pictures, tells the story, that there are individual letters and clusters of letters that make words, that text goes from left to right, and that the left page of a book is read before the right page. Writing skills develop as children have a real purpose for writing while they engage in role-playing. Writing letters while involved in the Post Office center, writing prescriptions while engaged in the Veterinary Office or Doctor's Office, and writing customers' orders while playing in the Pizza Restaurant provide children with meaningful experiences for using the written word. Every center has experiences designed to help children develop concepts of print.

Phonemic awareness can be developed while children are involved in literacy play centers. Teachers can help children to identify letter sounds associated with items in the various centers. As children role-play in the grocery store, teachers can introduce **b** for bag, **f** for food, and **l** for list. Rhyming words can be experienced through the books, songs, and finger plays teachers incorporate into the literacy play center themes.

Mathematical concepts and skills are promoted in meaningful ways through literacy play centers. Children count, use one-to-one correspondence, recognize numbers and shapes, write numerals, identify coins and dollar bills, classify, and seriate while role-playing. In the Shoe Store, children classify shoes

 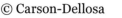

by type, match pairs of shoes, and arrange shoes by size. They write numerals as they create their grocery lists and use one-to-one correspondence as they provide customers with napkins, silverware, and cups in the Pizza Restaurant. An understanding of money develops as children pay for items purchased in the various centers. These experiences are embedded in the real-life experiences children have while role-playing.

Social studies concepts develop as children role-play. Mitchell (1934) stated that social studies curriculum for young children should be based on children's experiences and their discovery of the things in the culture of the world around them. Economic concepts of production, consumption, and distribution, for example, are developed through stocking shelves and buying products in the Grocery Store. As they role-play, children learn that goods must be produced or acquired. Such embryonic concepts are the foundation for children to build on as they learn more about the world (Seefeldt, 2005).

Social studies concepts are best developed through thematic units of study. Such units of study address children's curiosity about the real world by allowing them to investigate different careers and businesses. Ideas and concepts are expanded and consolidated through the literacy play centers since play and active learning are necessary for children to develop understanding (Vygotsky, 1986).

Children who are emotionally well-adjusted have a greater chance of early school success than those children who experience emotional difficulties (Raver, 2002). Providing opportunities for young children to develop positive social skills supports children's emotional development. Children learn attitudes, values, and social skills while participating in the literacy play centers. Cooperation, negotiation, turn taking, sharing, and conflict resolution emerge as children engage in role-playing. Literacy play centers provide rich settings in which children refine social skills, develop responsibility, and learn to follow rules.

Nonstereotypical views of roles in the workplace are developed as children assume the jobs people perform in the various centers. Children learn that doctor, nurse, veterinarian, postal worker, and other careers are available to both genders.

Physical development occurs as children are involved in the centers. Fine-motor skills improve as children manipulate objects and write their names, orders, bills, and receipts. Children use gross-motor skills as they pull a wagon to deliver pizza or flower orders, carry large objects, and bag groceries.

Planning and Preparation

Successful use of literacy play centers requires careful planning and preparation. It is essential to allow sufficient time in the daily schedule so that children will have a large block of uninterrupted time to play in the center. Allot at least thirty minutes a day, three days a week.

After establishing the daily schedule, the next step is to select a location in the classroom for a center. The type of literacy play center will influence the location. The Florist Shop, for example, requires sunlight for the plants that children will be growing, while the Fast-Food Restaurant, Pizza Restaurant, and Bakery need to be located near the Housekeeping center.

Once the location has been selected, evaluate existing furniture, props, and materials to determine what can be used in the center. Read the list of suggested props and materials provided in this book for each center. Check off what items are available and decide which props and materials you will need to obtain or create. Incorporate large pieces of classroom furniture within the centers. Use tables as store counters or exam tables for doctor or veterinary offices. Incorporate furniture from the Housekeeping center into a restaurant (Fast-Food or Pizza). Use existing shelves in the Grocery Store or Shoe Store. Include small cubbies as mail slots for the Post Office and for storing the safe-deposit boxes for the Bank.

You can use blocks, plastic foods, plastic containers, and manipulatives in various literacy play centers. Designate blocks as the lumber for the Home Improvement Store, use plastic food in the Pizza Restaurant or Grocery Store, and incorporate plastic containers into the Veterinary Office. You may need to modify or adapt some material. The creative use of existing furniture and materials is only limited by your imagination and your students' imagination.

Additional sources of props and materials include families, community resources, and the Internet. Families may be able to provide generic materials as well as materials related to specific literacy play themes. At the beginning of the year, a letter can be sent to families asking them to save and send in empty paper-roll tubes, empty cans, and plastic trays. These generic items can then be incorporated into many different themes.

Families can also contribute items for specific literacy play centers. Old shoes, shoe boxes, shoelaces, and shoe polish can be sent in for the Shoe Store. Families may have old bolts, washers, screws, tape measures, and rulers to contribute to a Home Improvement Store. Encourage donations of empty cereal and cracker boxes, and milk and egg cartons for the Grocery Store. Inform families of the need for items for literacy play centers. Providing suggestions for possible contributions while encouraging families to think about additional items to contribute may extend the literacy play centers in unexpected ways. You can use the letter on page 155 to request materials or include requests for materials in your monthly newsletter.

 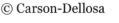

Many community stores and agencies are willing to donate materials to educational programs. If they are unable to donate materials, many stores will offer discount prices. Restaurants will often donate place mats, cups, paper plates, and napkins with their logos on them. Take-out food containers and paper bags are additional items that may be obtained from restaurants. Home improvement centers may donate scrap lumber and small pieces of leftover plastic pipe. They may be willing to provide carpet squares and wallpaper samples or wallpaper books. It is important to allow sufficient time for the stores and agencies to collect or save the materials requested.

Appliance boxes and other large cardboard boxes can be obtained from appliance and/or home improvement stores as well as grocery stores. Since many of these stores now collapse the boxes and recycle them, it will be necessary to ask the store manager to save the boxes and make arrangements to pick them up on a specific day.

For the first three centers, you will probably be collecting, assembling, and arranging most of the props and materials. Once children have experience in the literacy play centers, they can help organize and arrange future centers.

Children can also help create props to be used in the centers. They can paint large boxes with tempera paint if you draw the outlines with markers. They can draw and paint scenery and create labels and signs. When children are involved in creating the props and center, they have a sense of ownership and are more likely to be excited about playing in the center.

In addition to family and community resources, the Internet is a valuable source. Using a search engine (Google, Yahoo, AltaVista, etc.), you can locate and print images to use on word cards, charts, finger plays, and signs. Environmental print can be downloaded, printed, and displayed. Songs, finger plays, books, ideas, and lesson plans for themes are widely available on the Internet.

In addition to the furniture and props needed in the centers, you must also acquire literacy materials to use. Children's literature should be an integral part of literacy play centers. Use fiction and nonfiction children's literature with every center. Select books most appropriate for children in your classroom. This requires you to read a variety of books associated with the theme. Libraries have a wealth of books you can borrow. If a library does not have a book available, interlibrary loans are possible. The time necessary to obtain books through interlibrary loan varies with the library and book requested. Therefore, begin your search for books in sufficient time to obtain the desired texts.

Other print materials that should be placed in the literacy play center include pamphlets, magazines, flyers, and brochures. These can be obtained from local businesses and offices.

Create print specific to each center. Incorporate a classroom word wall with the literacy play centers. A word wall is a place in the classroom where you display words (Cunningham, 2004). Each center will have specific vocabulary associated with the theme. Build a word wall in your classroom by dividing an area into 26 spaces and placing both uppercase and lowercase forms of each letter in alphabetical order (Bauer, Walcavich, and Nipps, 2006). Allow enough room under each letter to display several word cards. As each center is introduced and used, add new words to the word wall. Leave the words from each center on the word wall throughout the year.

Words for the centers are in boldface in the instructions for each center. Make several copies of your own word cards on paper or index cards. Additional word cards for the centers, based on children's interests, can be added. All word cards should contain a rebus to help emergent readers identify the word. Include environmental print for word cards when possible. Laminate or use clear contact paper on the word cards to make them durable. Then, place them on the word wall.

In addition to word cards, create two name cards for each child in the program. Place one set of name cards on the word wall. The remaining name cards will be used in various ways in the literacy play centers. Children can use them as models to create their own name tags. They can also use them to select a role to play in the center.

Include numerous types of charts in the different centers. These may be written on chart paper or poster board. Purchase a pocket chart to work with index cards, sentence strips, or card stock cut to create various text props.

Incorporate finger plays, poems, and songs related to the theme. Create rebus charts of the finger plays, poems, and songs provided in this book to use with children. Leave a space between the lines when writing the text. Write key words from the text on individual cards so children can match word cards to the words on the chart. Use the charted finger plays, poems, and songs repeatedly during the time the literacy play center is in operation. The more exposure children have to written words, the more meaningful they become.

Download pictures of people working for each role needed in a literacy play center. Then, place these pictures next to each word naming a role. A picture of a cashier next to the word **cashier** would be one of the roles in the Grocery Store.

Creating role charts for each center provides a means for children to select the role they will play. Role charts help children remember the various jobs involved in the theme of the literacy play center and will reduce or eliminate confusion and disagreements among children.

Other charts that convey information relevant to the theme support literacy development. In the Florist Shop, a chart showing a variety of labeled flower arrangements, such as a Valentine Bouquet or the parts of a plant chart, provide meaningful written materials for children to use. The Veterinary Office can have a chart of pets with each animal labeled.

Every center will require signs unique to the theme. There will, however, be some signs that can be used in most centers, such as Enter, Exit, Open, and Closed. Determine the signs necessary and appropriate for each literacy play center. Many of the signs for the centers in this book have been suggested. There may be additional signs that you decide to incorporate. Laminate or cover all signs in the instructions with contact paper to make them durable. Include pictures on every sign to support children's reading.

The time and effort to make the literacy elements durable will benefit you in the long run. You will find that after the initial development of a literacy play center, preparation will decrease when the center is used again.

    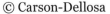

Preparing Children

It is critical that children have concrete experiences to build background knowledge to facilitate their play. One of the best ways to accomplish this is through field trips. Arrange to take children on a field trip to locations associated with the literacy play centers. If a field trip is not feasible, the next best experience is to invite people from the community into the classroom. Imagine the excitement and learning as children visit a postal worker or interact with a veterinarian in the classroom. Once this foundation is established, you can provide experiences to expand children's concepts.

Careful preparation for field trips or visitors is necessary. Determine what children should learn from these experiences. Discuss this information with the individual(s) involved in the field trip or classroom visit and decide how best to accomplish this.

Develop rules with children for participation in the centers by conducting a group meeting. The rules established should be generic in order to address any literacy play center setup in the room. Any rules specific to a particular center can be addressed when the center is introduced to children.

Initiate a discussion about appropriate behavior while playing in the centers. Help children create rules. All rules should be stated in positive terms to help children focus on acceptable behaviors rather than negative behaviors. Establish a limited number of rules. Generally, create no more than five rules and address broad expectations. Suggested rules include:

1. Sign up for a role.

2. Be kind and cooperate with your friends.

3. Use the materials carefully.

4. Use indoor voices.

5. Put all materials away where they belong when done playing.

Write the rules on a chart and post it next to the center.

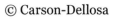

Implementing Literacy Play Centers

Introducing the Centers

There are some general procedures suggested to introduce any literacy play center theme. These procedures help children develop an understanding of the theme and extend their literacy experiences.

Build on children's personal experiences as well as experiences from the field trip and/or visitors. Engage them in a conversation about the center. Language is a means for children to make experiences meaningful. Vygotsky emphasized the importance of language in children's cognitive development (1986). Instead of directing children to raise their hand if they have ever been to a grocery store, pizza shop, or shoe store, ask open-ended questions to promote discussion. Then, ask follow up questions to expand on their recollection. Try to involve as many children as possible in the discussion. This will help build children's listening and speaking skills.

After the conversation about what children already know about how a particular store works and operates, extend their knowledge by reading one of the books from the book list. While reading aloud, be sure to stop and reinforce the new vocabulary (for example, **clerk**, **manager**, **stethoscope**). Discuss the new information found in each book and relate it to what children previously shared. This will help expand children's vocabulary and add to their developing schema about the new literacy play center.

Once children have a basic understanding of the new center, introduce it by showing them the name of the center written on a sign. Read the name of the center and ask children to read it. Invite them to walk into the new center and take them on a tour. Point out the different areas that have been established. Show them the props and materials that have been assembled for this center. Tell them the name of the item, show them the label, and encourage them to read it aloud. Demonstrate how to use the prop and place it back where it belongs in the center. Point out the importance of using the materials correctly and returning them to their special places. Allow enough time to share all of the props and materials. This may take more than one session, depending on children's interest and attentiveness.

After sharing the props and materials, show children the chart listing the roles available in the literacy play center. Help children identify the roles by examining the pictures next to the words and reading all of the different roles. Count the number of roles available. Point out that this is the number of children that can play in the center at one time.

Explain that children are to use their name cards to sign up for a role. Model how to select a role by placing a name card next to the picture word card of a particular role. Read the name card and the role with children again.

Ask for volunteers to choose which role they would like to play in the center. Select as many volunteers as there are roles to play and encourage each child to model what he or she will do when playing that role. Remind other children to watch closely because everyone will have a chance to pick and play a role. Encourage children to have fun.

Every child in the program should have opportunities to be involved in the center and to assume each role available during the time that the literacy play center is open. You can record, on a simple checklist, children's names and their roles each time the center is open. Using this information, you can encourage children to participate in the literacy play center and to assume different roles.

You may then choose to review the rules for center participation that were previously charted and ask if there are any questions. When all of the questions have been answered, place the Open sign in the center.

Procedures While the Center Is Open

Since the literacy play centers are an integral part of the curriculum, there are other activities that should be ongoing while each center is open. These activities include ways to build literacy using the word cards, the word wall, and the charted finger plays and songs.

Activities to Build Letter Recognition
Letter Hunt

Provide children with plastic magnifying glasses or make a set by cutting a circle out of construction paper and gluing plastic wrap inside the circle. Tell them that they are detectives who must find all of the words that begin with a certain letter in each center. While they are in the Grocery Store, children can be on the lookout for all food items that begin with **B** (**beans**, **bananas**), **F** (**Fritos,**® **fruit**, **fish**), and **L** (**lemons**, **lemonade**). Adjust the list to match the items that children have collected. In the Pizza Restaurant, children should look for items that begin with **P** (**pizza**, **pepperoni**), **M** (**mozzarella**, **menu**), **T** (**timer**, **tongs**), and **S** (**salt**, **soda**). You can also direct children to find words that begin with the same letters that were introduced in the previous centers.

Letter Construction

Write a large capital letter on a piece of construction paper for each letter being introduced in the literacy play center. Place bags of buttons, fruit-flavored ring cereal, or other materials that begin with the letter near the paper. Direct children to glue the buttons around the letter **B** or the "fruit loops" around the letter **F**.

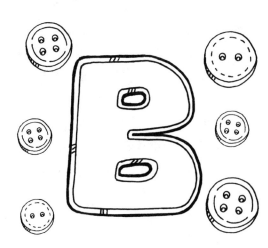

Magnetic Letters

Provide cookie sheets and magnetic letters so children can practice matching individual letters to the letters in the words and labels in each center.

Name Recognition

Provide alphabet-letter cookie cutters and colorful play dough for children to practice making their names and the names of their classmates. They can also reproduce words used in the centers.

Letter Sorts

Divide a manila file folder into two columns and print a large, uppercase letter and its matching lower-case letter at the top of each column. Attach a resealable plastic bag to the back of the folder. Select word cards from the centers and show children how to look at the beginning letter of the words. Sort all of the words that begin with the same letter by placing the words that begin alike under that letter on the file folder. Make a file folder for all 26 letters so that children will have an opportunity to practice sorting words that begin with each alphabet letter.

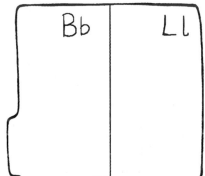

Finger Plays, Songs, and Poems

Laminate the finger plays, songs, and poems that you write on chart paper. Children can circle the letters that they are working on using an erasable marker.

Word Walls

There are numerous ways to incorporate the word wall into the daily routine. Encourage children to read the word wall as a large group during the opening activities. Appoint one child to be the leader. She can use a pointer to indicate which words she wants the class to read, or she can choose her favorite letter and ask everyone to read all of the words from the wall that begin with that letter. Children can chant all of the words on the word wall or chant all of the words that start with a specific letter. Children can play a game of I Spy. You would say, "I spy something that holds groceries" (bag) or "I spy something used to pound in nails" (hammer). Then, children would try to guess what you spied (Bauer, Walcavich, and Nipps, 2006).

You should also make multiple copies of the word cards listed in the centers so that children can match them to the words on the word wall independently or with a friend. Children can be encouraged to use the word cards in the writing center.

Word Sorts

Make another set of manila file folders like the ones described for the Letter Sorts (page 17), but this time glue a word card at the top of each column. Children may match the words that begin with the same letter and attempt to read the words aloud to a friend or teacher.

Read the Room

In addition to reading the word wall, encourage children to read the room. Model this by reading aloud the finger plays, poems, and songs that are displayed in the room. The helper of the day could lead the class in reciting one or more finger plays or poems or in singing a song while pointing to the words.

Concepts of Print

Providing a variety of books from the center book lists and encouraging children to look at the books in the centers will help them develop concepts of print. Because magazines, pamphlets, and other forms of printed material are available, children have opportunities to be exposed to a variety of text. They will also discover that there are different types of print media to read, enhancing their book-handling skills and concepts of how print works.

Environmental Print Book

Make a logo book using environmental print from the different centers. Create a 5–10 page book, place one product logo on each page, and encourage children to read the book (Bauer, Walcavich, and Nipps, 2006).

Activities to Build Mathematical Skills and Concepts

In addition to literacy skills, there are several ways that you can integrate activities to build children's math skills. These skills include number recognition, counting skills, shape identification, classification, and seriation.

Number Recognition and Counting

Reinforce number recognition and counting skills by providing games or activities based on the numbers that have been introduced in the centers. While the Grocery Store is open, label three paper grocery bags with the numbers 1, 2, and 3. Provide beanbags or soft balls that children can toss into the bags. Direct them to say which bag they plan to aim for by announcing that number. Play this game with small groups of children, and after each child has had a turn, direct the group to count how many objects ended up in each bag. This activity will also help improve their hand-eye coordination. While the Sporting Goods Store is open, set up 10 cups numbered 1 through 10 and ask children to put the correct number of golf tees in each cup. When all of the golf tees are in the cups, instruct children to count the total number of tees in each cup.

Shape Identification

While the Pizza Restaurant is open, reinforce the concepts of triangle and circle by playing a game of Musical Shapes. Cut out circles and triangles from construction paper and laminate them. Randomly arrange these shapes on the floor in the classroom. Explain to children that you will play some music, and when the music stops, they must stand on a shape. Ask children who are on circles to turn around twice and children on triangles to jump up and down three times. While the Post Office is open, review circles, triangles, squares, and rectangles by playing Twisted Shapes. Spread a clear shower curtain on the floor and attach different colorful circles, squares, rectangles, and triangles. Create a spinner with the same colorful shapes on it. Have children take turns moving the spinner and placing a foot or hand on a matching shape on the shower curtain.

Classification and Seriation

In the Sporting Goods store, children can sort golf tees and golf balls by color. In the Grocery Store, children can classify food according to how it is stored—refrigerator or cupboard. In the Home Improvement Store, children can seriate paint samples by color gradation and sandpaper by texture from smooth to rough.

 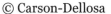

Coordinating with Other Existing Classroom Centers

Coordinate the activities that children do in the other classroom centers with the literacy centers. For example, while the Pizza Restaurant is open, children can make chefs' hats in the Art center, listen to a pizza-related book at the Listening center, draw and dictate a story about their favorite kind of pizza in the Writing center, and play the triangle in the Music center while singing the "Pizza Song." When the Post Office is open, children can create their own stamps out of potatoes in the Art center or dictate a message to write on a postcard in the Writing center.

Documenting Children's Learning

Pictures are worth a thousand words. Take several photos of children as they play in the centers. Digital pictures or film camera snapshots can be used to create documentation panels showcasing children at work. These panels are easy to create. Begin by sharing the pictures with children and asking them to explain what is happening in each picture. Record their explanations. Write the name of the literacy play center on the top of a poster or display board. Arrange pictures with children's explanations on this board. After sharing the documentation panel with all of the children, display it in the classroom.

If possible, videotape children as they engage in the literacy play centers. They will enjoy seeing themselves play. Sharing the videotape with parents gives them the opportunity to see their children actively involved in learning.

Closing the Literacy Play Centers

During the last week that each center is open, plan how to bring closure and celebrate children's learning. Look over the center book list and allow time to discuss the books that have been read, as well as share other books that may not have been read aloud. Record children's literature incorporated in each center to provide initial books to use next time.

Prepare the documentation panel so it can be displayed after the center is closed. Invite children to draw their favorite part of the center and create a mural. Encourage children to sign their artwork. Conduct a shared writing activity so that children will have an opportunity to tell about their favorite activities at the center. Post this story next to the mural.

Hang up a Going out of Business sign so children will know that the center is about to close. Write personal thank-you notes to businesses that provided props or materials. You should also have children send thank-you notes to the community agencies and stores that donated materials to the program. One option is to create and present each business with a large thank-you poster featuring pictures of children engaged in using the materials. This provides the agencies or stores with an opportunity to display the poster and show the community their contributions to children's education.

Invite children to help dismantle the center and store the props and materials. Clear plastic containers large enough to hold the materials work well for storage. Storage suggestions are provided for each center. Large manila envelopes can be used to store the literacy materials. Return borrowed props or materials, if necessary.

The word cards should remain on the word wall. Chart-paper finger plays, poems, and songs from the center can still be displayed after the center is closed.

 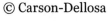

Literacy Play Centers Chart

Literacy Play Center	Letters/Sounds	Literacy Skills	Math Skills	Assessments
Grocery Store September	**Introduce:** B–bag; F–food; L–list	**Oral Language:** Conversation; phonemic awareness **Reading:** Beginning sounds and letters; environmental print; logos; concepts of print; book-handling skills	Classifying food products; recognizing the numerals 1, 2, 3; using money to pay for groceries	• Oral Language Rating Scale • Book-Handling Checklist • Socialization Skills Rating Scale
Pizza Restaurant October	**Introduce:** P–pizza; M–menu, T–tomato; S–soda and straw **Reinforce:** F–flour; B–bake	**Oral Language:** Conversation; phonemic awareness **Reading:** Beginning sounds and letters; environmental print; rebus menus **Written Language:** Writing classmates' orders; creating name tags, store signs, menus, and bills	Introduce shapes—circle and triangle; introduce measurement with measuring cups and spoons; recognizing numerals by reading the timer; introduce dollars and pennies; using money to pay for food	• Alphabet Knowledge • Shape Recognition • Oral Language Rating Scale • Book-Handling Checklist • Socialization Skills Rating Scale
Fast-Food Restaurant November	**Introduce:** K–ketchup; H–hamburger; E–exit` **Reinforce:** P–pickle; M–mustard; F–french fries	**Oral Language:** Conversation; phonemic awareness **Reading:** Beginning sounds and letters; environmental print; rhyming words; rebus menus **Written Language:** Writing food orders, bills, and name tags	Counting food items for customers; counting money; reading the timer; using money to pay for food	• Number Recognition • Oral Language Rating Scale • Book-Handling Checklist • Socialization Skills Rating Scale

Literacy Play Center	Letters/Sounds	Literacy Skills	Math Skills	Assessments

Doctor's Office
December
	Introduce:
	D–doctor; N–nurse;
	C–cold; I–itchy and in;
	X–X-ray; Q–Q-tips®; O–out
	Reinforce:
	F–flu; H–hurt and
	healthy; P–patient, S–sick
		Oral Language:
		Conversation; phonemic
		awareness
		Reading:
		Beginning sounds and let-
		ters; environmental print;
		alliteration; rhyming words
		Written Language:
		Writing prescriptions,
		patient notes, appointment
		cards, name tags, and
		sign-in sheet
			Reading charts and
			numbers on
			thermometers and scales;
			counting pills for
			prescriptions
				• Alphabet Knowledge
				• Emergent and Early
				  Writing Rubric
				• Number Recognition
				• Socialization Skills
				  Rating Scale

Shoe Store
January
	Introduce:
	O–open; V–Velcro®;
	R–rectangle
	Reinforce:
	N–newspaper; C–clerk;
	S–shoes, sandal, socks,
	and sneakers; P–purse;
	B–boots; Q–question mark
		Oral Language:
		Conversation; phonemic
		awareness; color
		recognition
		Reading:
		Beginning sounds and
		letters; environmental print;
		question mark
		Written Language:
		Writing customers' bills,
		price tags, name tags, and
		question marks
			Using money; reading
			numbers on rulers;
			sizing shoes; matching
			and graphing pairs of
			shoes; identifying most
			and least; estimating;
			measuring feet;
			recognizing rectangles
				• Book-Handling Checklist
				• Oral Language
				  Rating Scale
				• Socialization Skills
				  Rating Scale

Veterinary Office February	**Introduce:** A–animal **Reinforce:** B–bird; D–dog; C–cat; P–pet; V–Vet	**Oral Language:** Conversation; phonemic awareness **Reading:** Beginning sounds and letters; rhyming words; environmental print; onsets and rimes **Written Language:** Writing charts and prescriptions	One-to-one correspondence; matching size of cages to animals; reading numbers on scales and thermometers	• Alphabet Knowledge • Rhyming Words • Shape Recognition • Socialization Skills Rating Scale

Literacy Play Center	Letters/Sounds	Literacy Skills	Math Skills	Assessments
Barbershop/Hair Salon March	**Introduce:** G–gel; W–wig **Reinforce:** C–comb; H–hair; L–lotion; N–nail; P–polish; B–barber; R–razor	**Oral Language:** Conversation; phonemic awareness **Reading:** Beginning sounds and letters; environmental print **Written Language:** Writing/dictating story about first trip to barbershop/hair salon; writing name tags and bills for customers	Classifying hair products; using money to pay for products; pricing hair products; sequencing	• Emergent and Early Writing Rubric • Socialization Skills Rating Scale
Post Office April	**Introduce:** Z–ZIP code; J–junk mail **Reinforce:** B–bill; P–package and postage; S–stamp; L–letter; M–mail; E–enter; A–address	**Oral Language:** Conversation; phonemic awareness **Reading:** Beginning sounds and letters; environmental print; reading addresses, postcards, and letters **Written Language:** Writing postcards, letters, numbers, and name tags; designing stamps	Recognizing numbers by weighing packages; using dollar bills, quarters, and pennies to buy postal products; matching letters to envelopes	• Alphabet Knowledge • Number Recognition • Emergent and Early Writing Rubric • Socialization Skills Rating Scale
Florist Shop May	**Introduce:** Y–yellow **Reinforce:** F–flowers; P–plants; D–delivery; R–rose; G–garden	**Oral Language:** Conversation; phonemic awareness **Reading:** Beginning sounds and letters; environmental print; color recognition **Written Language:** Writing orders, bills, and name tags	Counting flowers; classifying flowers by color; using money to pay	• Syllable Recognition • Rhyming Words • Socialization Skills Rating Scale

    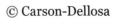

Literacy Play Center	Letters/Sounds	Literacy Skills	Math Skills	Assessments
Sporting Goods Store June	**Introduce:** U–umbrella **Reinforce:** J–jump rope; K–kite; M–mitt; B–bat and ball; G–golf; Y–yo-yo; R–racket	**Oral Language:** Conversation; phonemic awareness **Reading:** Beginning sounds and letters; environmental print; reading sports logos and rebus signs; syllables; rhyming words **Written Language:** Writing customer orders and bills	Classifying sports equipment and clothes; seriating, counting, and recognizing numerals through 10; using money to pay	• Alphabet Knowledge • Oral Language Rating Scale • Book-Handling Checklist • Syllable Recognition • Socialization Skills Rating Scale
Home Improvement Store	**Reinforce:** H–hammer; I–improve; T–tools; L–lumber; B–belt	**Oral Language:** Conversation; phonemic awareness **Reading:** Beginning sounds and letters; environmental print; advertisements and labels **Written Language:** Writing orders and signs	Seriating and counting money; classifying; matching sizes; using money to pay; square shape	All assessments
Bank	**Reinforce:** B–bank; A–ATM; M–money; D–dollar and dime; P–penny; N–nickel; T–teller; C–cash; Z–zero	**Oral Language:** Conversation; phonemic awareness **Reading:** Beginning sounds and letters; environmental print; names of classmates; bank forms **Written Language:** Writing deposit slips, withdrawal slips, and checks	Recognizing money, using an adding machine	All assessments

Literacy Play Center	Letters/Sounds	Literacy Skills	Math Skills	Assessments
Bakery	**Reinforce:** D–doughnut, dozen; B–baker; C–cake, coffee, and cocoa; G–glazed	**Oral Language:** Conversation; phonemic awareness **Reading:** Beginning sounds and letters; environmental print; recipes and menus **Written Language:** Writing customer orders, designing place mats, and pricing baked goods	Circle shape, concept of dozen and half dozen; using money to pay for baked goods; measuring; using a timer	All assessments
Optometrist's Office	**Reinforce:** U–up; D–down; O–Optometrist; P–patient; G–glasses, green; F–frames; B–brown, blue; H–hazel	**Oral Language:** Conversation; phonemic awareness; directionality **Reading:** Beginning sounds and letters; environmental print; color recognition; reading patient charts **Written Language:** Writing patient orders, bills, and receipts	Counting to 11; recognizing numerals; using position words	All Assessments
Movie Theater	**Reinforce:** M–movie; T–ticket; P–popcorn, pop, pot; U–usher; C–candy	**Oral Language:** Conversation; phonemic awareness **Reading:** Beginning and ending sounds and letters; reading movie ads and ticket stubs; environmental print; elements of a story **Written Language:** Writing name tags, movie reviews, movie posters, tickets, and signs	Counting money; pricing candy; rating movies on a scale from 1 to 4 stars; using money to pay	Oral Retelling

Letters/Sounds Index

Letter/Sound	Words for Word Wall (Literacy Play Center)	Words to Reinforce Letter/Sound (Literacy Play Center)
A	animal (Veterinary Office)	address (Post Office)
		ATM (Bank)
B	bag (Grocery Store)	bake (Pizza Restaurant)
		bat, ball (Sporting Goods Store)
		boots (Shoe Store)
		bill (Post Office)
		bird (Veterinary Office)
		barber (Barbershop/Hair Salon)
		belt (Home Improvement Store)
		bank (Bank)
		baker (Bakery)
		brown, blue (Optometrist's Office)
C	cold (Doctor's Office)	cat (Veterinary Office)
		comb (Barbershop/Hair Salon)
		clerk (Shoe Store)
		cash (Bank)
		cake, coffee, cocoa (Bakery)
		candy (Movie Theater)
D	doctor (Doctor's Office)	dog (Veterinary Office)
		delivery (Florist Shop)
		dollar, dime (Bank)
		dozen, doughnut (Bakery)
		down (Optometrist's Office)
E	exit (Fast-Food Restaurant)	enter (Post Office)
F	food (Grocery Store)	french fries (Fast-Food Restaurant)
		flour (Pizza Restaurant)
		flu (Doctor's Office)
		flowers (Florist Shop)
		frames (Optometrist's Office)
G	gel (Barbershop/Hair Salon)	golf (Sporting Goods Store)
		garden (Florist Shop)
		green, glasses (Optometrist's Office)
		glazed (Bakery)

Letter/Sound	Words for Word Wall (Literacy Play Center)	Words to Reinforce Letter/Sound (Literacy Play Center)
H	hamburger (Fast-Food Restaurant)	hurt, healthy (Doctor's Office)
		hair (Barbershop/Hair Salon)
		hammer (Home Improvement Store)
		hazel (Optometrist's Office)
I	itchy, in (Doctor's Office)	improve (Home Improvement Store)
J	junk mail (Post Office)	jump rope (Sporting Goods Store)
K	ketchup (Fast-Food Restaurant)	kite (Sporting Goods Store)
L	list (Grocery Store)	lotion (Barbershop/Hair Salon)
		letter (Post Office)
		lumber (Home Improvement Store)
M	menu (Pizza Restaurant)	mustard (Fast-Food Restaurant)
		mitt (Sporting Goods Store)
		mail (Post Office)
		money (Bank)
		movie (Movie Theater)
N	nurse (Doctor's Office)	newspaper (Shoe Store)
		nail (Barbershop/Hair Salon)
		nickel (Bank)
O	out (Doctor's Office)	open (Shoe Store)
P	pizza (Pizza Restaurant)	pickle (Fast-Food Restaurant)
		package, postage (Post Office)
		patient (Doctor's Office)
		penny (Bank)
		pet (Veterinary Office)
		plants (Florist Shop)
		popcorn, pop, pot (Movie Theater)
		purse (Shoe Store)
		polish (Barbershop/Hair Salon)
Q	Q-tips® (Doctor's Office)	question mark (Shoe Store)
R	rectangle (Shoe Store)	rose (Florist Shop)
		racket (Sporting Goods Store)
		razor (Barbershop/Hair Salon)
S	soda, straw (Pizza Restaurant)	sick (Doctor's Office)
		stamp (Post Office)
		shoes, sandal, socks, and sneakers (Shoe Store)
T	tomato (Pizza Restaurant)	teller (Bank)
		tools (Home Improvement Store)
		ticket (Movie Theater)

Letter/Sound	Words for Word Wall (Literacy Play Center)	Words to Reinforce Letter/Sound (Literacy Play Center)
U	umbrella (Sporting Goods Store)	up (Optometrist's Office)
		usher (Movie Theater)
V	Velcro® (Shoe Store)	vet (Veterinary Office)
W	wig (Barbershop/Hair Salon)	
X	X-ray (Doctor's Office)	
Y	yellow (Florist Shop)	yo-yo (Sporting Goods Store)
Z	ZIP code (Post Office)	zero (Bank)

 # Math Skills Index

Math Skill/Concept	Literacy Play Center	Activity
Classification	Grocery Store	Sorting and shelving grocery products
Classification	Barbershop/Hair Salon	Sorting hair products
Classification	Sporting Goods Store	Sorting sports equipment and clothes
Classification	Florist Shop	Sorting flowers by color
Classification	Home Improvement Store	Sort products by department
Matching	Veterinary Office	Selecting appropriately sized cages for pets
Matching	Shoe Store	Matching pairs of shoes and socks
Matching	Post Office	Matching letters to envelopes
Matching	Home Improvement Store	Matching screws, washers, and bolts
Number Recognition	Grocery Store	Numbers 1, 2, 3
Number Recognition	Pizza Restaurant, Fast-Food Restaurant, Bakery	Reading numbers on a timer
Number Recognition	Doctor's Office, Veterinary Office	Reading numerals on thermometers, scales
Number Recognition	Post Office	Reading numbers on a scale
Number Recognition	Shoe Store	Reading numbers on the foot rulers and finding the matching sized shoes
Number Recognition	Sporting Goods Store	Numbers 1–10
Number Recognition	Bank	Adding numbers on an adding machine
Number Recognition	Optometrist's Office	Reading numbers in eye exam book

Math Skill/Concept	Literacy Play Center	Activity
Money Recognition	Grocery Store, Pizza Restaurant, Fast-Food Restaurant, Shoe Store, Barbershop/Hair Salon, Post Office, Florist Shop, Sporting Goods Store, Home Improvement Store, Bakery, Movie Theater	Using money to pay for products and services
Money Recognition	Home Improvement Store	Concept of penny, quarter, and dollar
Money Recognition	Bank	Concept of penny, nickel, dime, quarter, and dollar
Money Recognition	Movie Theater	Counting money
Shape Recognition	Pizza Restaurant	Circle and triangle
Shape Recognition	Shoe Store	Rectangle
Shape Recognition	Bakery	Circle
Shape Recognition	Home Improvement Store	Square
Shape Recognition	Movie Theater	Star shape
Concept of Number	Fast-Food Restaurant	Counting out the number of items that customers want
Concept of Number	Doctor's Office	Counting pills
Concept of Number	Barbershop/Hair Salon	Pricing hair products
Concept of Number	Florist Shop	Counting the correct number of flowers
Concept of Number	Bakery	Counting a dozen and a half dozen
Concept of Number	Sporting Goods Store	Counting up to 10
Concept of Number	Optometrist's Office	Counting to 11
Concept of Number	Movie Theater	Pricing candy
Number Quantity	Movie Theater	Rating movies from 1 to 4 stars
Measurement Skills	Shoe Store	Measuring feet
Measurement Skills	Pizza Restaurant, Bakery	Using measuring cups and spoons
Graphing	Shoe Store	Matching and graphing shoes
Concept of Most and Least	Shoe Store	Reading and interpreting the shoe graph
Estimation	Shoe Store	Predicting types of shoes that will appear most and least
One-to-One Correspondence	Veterinary Office	Placing one pet in one cage
Sequence	Barbershop/Hair Salon	Sequencing and numbering the steps involved in getting a haircut
Seriation Skills	Sporting Goods Store	Seriating balls by size
Seriation Skills	Home Improvement Store	Seriating shades of color from lightest to darkest

Grocery Store

Goals and Objectives for Children

1. To learn what a literacy play center is by playing at the Grocery Store and developing shared rules for participation in the center

2. To develop an understanding of how a grocery store operates through practice and simulation

3. To develop oral communication skills through role-playing various roles, such as store manager, shopper, bagger, cashier, delicatessen manager, dairy manager, meat manager, etc.

4. To develop concepts of print by reading food containers, matching coupons to actual grocery items, and reading the center books (page 33)

5. To reinforce book-handling skills by reading the various books at the center

6. To develop phonemic awareness of the **B** sound in **bag**, the **F** sound in **food**, and the **L** sound in **list**

7. To develop reading skills by reading environmental print and food item labels and logos

8. To develop writing skills by creating a grocery list and name tag

9. To develop math skills of classification by sorting grocery products, food labels, and logos, and placing like products in the same area in the grocery store

10. To develop the ability to select an appropriately sized bag for items purchased

11. To introduce children to the concept of purchasing products using money

12. To develop number recognition of the numbers 1, 2, and 3

13. To develop cooperative learning skills by interacting with other children at the Grocery Store

    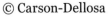

Props

- Empty food containers and boxes
- Grocery carts or baskets
- Scrap paper to stuff empty boxes
- Conveyor belt
- Variety of empty household product containers
- Foam or plastic trays
- Empty frozen food and dairy product containers
- Paper bags
- Cash register
- Play money
- Scale for weighing produce
- Table for deli counter, meat counter, bakery, produce, dairy products

Print Materials

- Center sign with the name of Grocery Store
- Newspaper ads for grocery stores
- Coupons (actual ones you have collected, as well as coupons you have made with product logos)
- Note pads for grocery lists, grocery lists with logos
- Name tags for cashier, store manager, and various department managers (meat, produce, dairy, etc.)
- Signs for Open/Closed, Exit, Hours of Operation
- Display signs for the store and for the various departments, such as Meat Department, Dairy, Frozen Foods, Produce, Bakery, Delicatessen, Beverages, etc.
- Blank labels to price grocery items
- File box or other coupon holder
- Assortment of food product labels
- Shopper Club discount cards
- Price signs and daily specials
- Rebus word cards for **B–bag**, **F–food**, and **L–list**
- Chart with pictures of the roles children can play in this center, including meat manager, the bakery manager, the delicatessen worker, the produce manager, stock clerks, store manager, and cashier
- "Food" finger play (page 36) written on chart paper (Leave two lines between each line of the song so children will have space to match the letters.)

      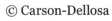

Writing Materials

- Pens, pencils, and markers

- Name tags

- Note pads

- Blank labels

- Price signs

Book List

- *Don't Forget the Bacon!* by Pat Hutchins (Gardners Books, 2001)
  A little boy tries to remember what his mother told him to get at the grocery store.

- *Grocery Store* by Angela Leeper (Heinemann, 2004)
  Looks at what the employees do in the different departments of a grocery store.

- *Signs at the Store* by Mary Hill (Children's Press, 2003)
  While at the grocery store with her father, Carly notices all of the signs posted for the shoppers.

- *Something Good* by Robert Munsch (Annick Press, 1990)
  This funny book is about a family's shopping trip to the grocery store.

- *A Visit to the Supermarket* by B. A. Hoena (Pebble Plus, 2004)
  Meet supermarket employees, look at the different departments they work in and the tools they use for their work.

- *Where Are You?* by Francesca Simon (Peachtree Publishers, 1998)
  Harry, a little puppy, runs around the grocery store following the wonderful smells and gets separated from his grandfather.

Storage Container

Use a large box or several plastic baskets to store all of the empty food products and containers. Store writing, print, and reading materials in brown paper bags.

Implementing the Grocery Store

Procedures:

Step 1   Visit local grocery stores to collect paper and plastic bags. Look at the various print materials that are displayed (department signs, weekly specials board or sign, etc.). If possible, arrange for your class to take a field trip to a grocery store.

Step 2   Collect as many empty food containers as possible. Send a letter home to parents asking them to save empty cereal and cracker boxes, plastic containers, snack bags, milk jugs, egg cartons, etc. Visit the local library to check out books. Feel free to check out books from the center book list (page 33), as well as other books about food.

Step 3   Download appropriate environmental print, logos, food images, and signs from the Internet. (Go to a search engine and type in *signs* or *cereals* to get an assortment of product logos). Use these to make signs for the store, as well as the word cards. Each word card should have a picture representing the word beside it. Obtain a large cardboard box from a local store and cut out one side to be used as a conveyor belt. Use black spray paint or markers to color it black. Cut out meat shapes from paper or use plastic food items and arrange them on foam trays and cover with plastic wrap. Sort the various food products to determine the number of categories. Put price tags on the items using only the numerals 1, 2, and 3.

Step 4   Choose an area in the classroom with shelves that could accommodate the grocery containers and products. Set up tables for the various departments. Hang the store sign and the department signs. Set up the conveyor belt on a table next to the cash register. Create a chart of the roles that children can play in this center by displaying pictures of a cashier, store manager, and as many department heads as the center can accommodate. Be sure to include customer as a role.

Step 5   Introduce this center by gathering children together in front of the Grocery Store sign. Show them a grocery bag filled with various food products. Tell children that **bag** begins with the **B** sound. Invite them to make the **B** sound aloud and write the word **bag** on a card next to a picture of a bag. Show children the word card for **bag** and ask a volunteer to read the card and place it on the word wall. Ask children if they can think of other words that begin with the **B** sound. Be sure to include the names of children in the class that begin with **B**. Take one item out of the bag and ask children to identify the product.

HINT: Include two items from each category in the bag. For example, cereal box, dairy product (butter tub, milk jug, etc.), bakery item (doughnut box, cookie bag, etc.), cracker box, meat, delicatessen package, etc. After children say the name of the product, show them the shelves, tables, and signs and ask them where they should place the first item and why it should go there. Follow this same procedure so that children have classified and placed in the appropriate site at least two items from each category.

Step 6 Generate a conversation about grocery stores by asking questions, such as *Where have you gone grocery shopping with your mom or dad? How did your mom or dad know what to buy?* If no one says they followed a list, introduce this idea by sharing a list.

HINT: Use logos and food images that you have downloaded to create a rebus shopping list of products that you believe your children are most familiar with and can easily recognize. Write the numeral that corresponds with how many of that item will be purchased. Only use 1, 2, or 3 at this point. Include a box where children can check off each item when they find it or laminate the lists and give children wipe-away markers to draw a line through each item after they find it.

Show the grocery list and tell children that **list** starts with **L**. Invite children to say the word **list** aloud and make the **L** sound. Show them the word card for **list** and place it on your word wall.

Grocery List

☐ bananas

☐ milk

☐ bread

☐ orange juice

Read the list with children and ask for a volunteer to find each item on the shelf or table and place it into a grocery cart or basket. Ask them what it means when a number 2 is in front of the picture of the bread. Model how to mark each item off the list after the item has been located and placed in the grocery cart.

Step 7 Include one item that will not be found on the shelves and explain that sometimes grocery shoppers can't find what they want and need to ask someone for help. Share the name tags that have been previously created for the store manager and other department heads. Share one name tag at a time and role-play how to ask a store employee for help. Tell children that when they are playing in the store, they will all have the opportunity to be a manager.

Store Manager
Produce Manager
Cashier

Step 8 Ask children what they need to do after they have found all of the groceries that they need. Show them the conveyor belt and ask a volunteer to place the items on the belt while you model the role of cashier and ring up the items on the cash register. Tell children that you are the cashier and point out your cashier name tag. Show how to find the price tag on the items and locate the matching numbers on the cash register. Tell children that now they have to pay for the groceries, but they could save money if they had discount coupons. Show them the file box with the coupons arranged in alphabetical order and model how to check to see if there are any matching coupons. Have the customer pay for the groceries and then give the money back for the coupon redemptions.

Step 9 During story time, share a story about grocery shopping from the center book list (page 33). Stress the parts of the story that relate to the process of grocery shopping. Remind children that tomorrow they will be able to play in the grocery store. Share the chart-paper finger play "Food" with students.

> Food
>
> I like food.
> So does my tummy.
> I like food.
> It tastes yummy!

Print the words **Food** and **food** on cards that children can match to the finger play on the chart. Point out that both cards say the same thing but are different in one way. Challenge children to figure out how the two words are different (one starts with an uppercase letter and one is written in lowercase). Call on volunteers to come to the chart and place the correct word card under the word on the chart. Accent the **F** sound and mention other words that children may know that begin with the **F** sound. Be sure to include the names of children in the class that begin with **F**. Place the food word card on the word wall. Briefly show children the other food and grocery-related books. Tell children that the books will be placed in the Grocery Store so that they can look at them before you read them aloud. Depending on the length of the story and children's attention spans, decide whether to share the list of rules for participation in literacy play centers now

 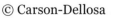

or at a later time. Just be sure to discuss and list expected behaviors before the center is opened to children.

Step 10 Before opening the Grocery Store to children, review the rules that have been posted in the classroom. Show them the grocery store chart and name the various roles that children can play. Tell them that the customer does not need a name tag and ask them why that is so. Tell them how many children can play in the center at one time and remind them that this center will be open for three to four weeks so that everyone will have the chance to shop in the Grocery Store. Review the word cards that have been introduced in this center.

Step 11 Collect the assessment materials that will be used in the Grocery Store and place them in a convenient location near the center. The first three instruments that you will use include the Book-Handling Skills Checklist (page 135), the Oral Language Rating Scale (page 136), and the Socialization Skills Rating Scale (137). Refer to pages 133–134 for tips and suggestions on how to use these in the center.

 # Pizza Restaurant

Goals and Objectives for Children

1. To develop an understanding of how a pizza restaurant operates through practice and simulation

2. To develop oral communication skills through role-playing various roles, such as waiter/waitress, shop owner or manager, customer, cook, or cashier

3. To develop oral-communication skills by answering the telephone and taking orders and by greeting and seating customers

4. To develop concepts of print by reading menus, tomato sauce cans, and other food containers, and by reading the center books (page 40)

5. To develop book handling skills by encouraging children to read the various books at the center

6. To develop phonemic awareness of the **P** sound in **pizza**, the **T** sound in **tomato**, the **S** sound in **soda** and **straws**, the **M** sound in **menu**, and to reinforce the **F** sound in **food** and the **B** sound in **bake** introduced in the Grocery Store

7. To develop reading skills by reading environmental print, reading and ordering from menus, and reading the center books (page 40)

8. To develop writing skills by creating name tags, filling out customers' food orders, and writing "bills" or checks for the customers

9. To develop math skills by practicing measuring and reading numbers on measuring cups and spoons and setting the timer for 20 minutes

10. To develop the ability to recognize a whole pizza as a circle and slices of pizza as triangle shaped

11. To develop the ability to recognize the dollar bill and the penny

12. To develop cooperative learning skills by interacting with other children at the Pizza Restaurant

Props

- Measuring cups and spoons
- Paper plates and straws
- Plastic cups, forks, and spoons
- Pizza pans
- Telephone
- Chef's hat and aprons
- Mixing bowls
- Empty yeast bags
- Cardboard pizza boxes
- Wagon or tricycle delivery vehicle
- Serving tray
- Cash register
- Play money

- Timer
- Tomato sauce cans
- Kitchen utensils (serving spoon, spatula, etc.)
- Place mats
- Rolling pin
- Dish towels
- Cardboard pizza circles
- Spaghetti, meatballs, and pepperoni (made out of yarn, play dough, or foam)
- Cheese made out of plastic strips
- Empty flour and salt bags or containers
- Insulated delivery bag
- Red felt circles

Print Materials

- Center sign with Pizza Restaurant (Leave a space in front to add a name later.)
- Signs for Open/Closed, Exit, Hours of Operation, No Smoking
- Menus and daily specials
- Reservation book
- Recipes
- Bills/checks
- Suggestion box
- Rebus word cards for **P–pizza**, **T–tomato**, **S–soda, and M–menu**

- Chart with pictures of the roles children can play in this center, including waiter/waitress, restaurant owner or manager, customer, cook, or cashier
- Name tags for waiter/waitress, manager, cook, and cashier
- "Pizza" song (page 42) written on chart paper (Leave two lines between each line of the song so children will have space to match the letters.)

Writing Materials

- Pens, pencils, and markers
- Order pads
- Name tags
- Bills and receipts
- Note pads
- Reservation book

Book List

- *Let's Make Pizza* by Mary Hill (Children's Press, 2002)
  A little girl and her father go through the steps of making a pizza.

- *Little Nino's Pizzeria* by Karen Barbour (Voyager Books, 1990)
  Nino calls his son, Tony, the best helper in his pizza shop until he decides to open a bigger, fancier pizza shop.

- *The Little Red Hen Makes a Pizza* by Amy Walrod (Puffin Books, 2002)
  After the little red hen ate her last piece of bread, she decided to make a pizza. Who will help her?

- *Pete's a Pizza* by William Steig (HarperCollins, 1998)
  When Pete is in a bad mood, his dad decides to turn him into a pizza.

- *Pizza Pat* by Rita Golden Gelman (Random House Books for Young Readers, 1999)
  A rhyming cumulative story about Pat making a pizza.

- *The Pizza That We Made* by Joan Holub (Puffin Books, 2001)
  This book contains step-by-step illustrated directions for making a pizza.

- *Veggies on Our Pizza* by Chantelle B. Goodman (Pentland Press, 2002)
  An ABC book about all of the different vegetables that children want their moms to put on their pizza.

- *What Do You Want on Your Pizza?* by William Boniface (Price Stern Sloan, Inc., 2000)
  This board book comes with cardboard pictures of actual toppings that children can fit on the slices of pizza.

Storage Container

A wagon that doubles as a pizza delivery vehicle can also be used as the storage container. Plastic and paper utensils, pizza pans, and props can be stored in empty pizza boxes (these can usually be obtained from "real" pizza restaurants for free). Cooking and baking utensils can be placed inside the large mixing bowl. Writing materials, note pads, order pads, and aprons can be kept inside the chef's hat.

Implementing the Pizza Restaurant

Procedures:

Step 1   Visit local pizza restaurants or take-outs to collect sample menus, pizza boxes and circles, napkins, and packages of red peppers, salt, and pepper. Look at the different types of literacy materials that are displayed (signs, posters, menus, order forms, name tags, etc.).

Step 2   Collect or create as many props, print, and writing materials as possible from the props and materials lists. Visit the local library to check out books. Be sure to get some cookbooks, as well as picture books.

Step 3   Download appropriate environmental print, food images, and signs from the Internet. Gather the cooking supplies, pizza-making materials, and restaurant props (chairs and tables). Use the food images to create a rebus menu, word cards (page 39), reservation book, bills/receipts, and order slips. Use environmental print logos to design place mats.

Step 4   Choose an area in the classroom close to the Housekeeping center so children will have access to the stove, sink, and refrigerator. (If you do not have an established Housekeeping center, obtain large boxes and turn one into a stove with an oven, another one into a refrigerator, and the third one into a sink. Cut a circular area into the top side of one box large enough to accommodate a big bowl and place the bowl into it to serve as a sink.) Hang a big sign that says _____'s Pizza Restaurant to pique children's interest.

Step 5   Introduce the center by gathering children together near the Housekeeping center. Point out the Pizza Restaurant sign and show children an empty pizza box. Ask if anyone knows what food item usually comes in a box like this? Lead them to say **pizza** by providing extra clues if necessary (for example, "This food has red sauce on it, and I like mine with pepperoni."). Point out the word **pizza** on the box and invite children to read the word aloud. Point out the beginning letter and make the **P** sound. Ask children if they see the word **pizza** somewhere else in the classroom. After they find the word on the sign, point to each letter in the word **pizza** on the sign and on the box. Invite children to read the word again. Tell them the blank space on the sign before the word **pizza** is the place where they will get to write the name of their Pizza Restaurant.

Step 6   Generate a discussion about pizza by asking questions like *What do you like on your pizza?* (tell children that you like **pepperoni**, stressing the **P** sound) and *Where does your family buy their pizzas? What shape is pizza?* (A whole pizza is usually circular or round and individual pieces are usually shaped like triangles.)

Draw both shapes on the board and hold up the round pizza circle or pan and a triangular piece of construction paper decorated like a slice of pizza.

Sing the chart paper song, "Pizza," with children. (Leave two lines in between each line of the song so children will have space to match the letters.)

Add the word card **pizza** to the word wall. Make individual letter cards for each letter in pizza so that children can match them to the printed letters of the song on chart paper. Children can do this activity now and later when they are in the Pizza Restaurant.

> Pizza
>
> (sing to the tune of "Bingo")
>
> P-I- Z- Z- A
>
> P -I- Z- Z- A
>
> P -I- Z- Z -A
>
> And Pizza is a pie–O!

Step 7 Open one of the pizza boxes used for storage and pull out the props one by one. Ask children to identify each prop and have everyone repeat the name of each object. Ask children what they would need to make pizza and show them the bag of **flour**. Point out the letter **F** at the beginning of the word **flour** and ask them to name that letter. Have everyone make the **F** sound and ask if anyone remembers other words that start with this same sound. Remind children that **flour** starts like **food**. Add the word card for **flour** to the word wall. Show children the following props: yeast packages, water bottle, bag of sugar, measuring cups and spoons, rolling pin, pizza pan, and various topping materials. Model how to put on the apron and the chef's hat. As you put on the chef's hat, arrange for the writing materials that were previously placed in the hat to fall out. Explain how to use each one and model how to make a name tag and to attach it so that all of the customers can see who is waiting on them.

Tell children that customers can either eat in the restaurant (show them the table and chairs and read the place mats that have been designed) or call in their orders. Customers can also pick up the orders themselves or have them delivered. Show children the area that has been established as the pickup counter. Model how to answer the phone, take down the order on the order tablet, and calculate the bill. Show children the wagon that will be used to deliver the pizza orders.

Step 8 Invite children to come into the Pizza Restaurant and help place all of the materials. Model how to make a pizza by reading the recipe and placing the white cardboard circle onto the round pizza pan. Ask children to identify the shape of the pan. Show them an empty tomato sauce can and point out the letter **T** at the beginning of the word **tomato**. Ask if anyone knows what letter

   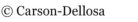

tomato starts with and link to the names of children and days of the week that begin with the **T** sound. Add the word card for **tomato** to the word wall. Show children the red felt circle that will be used for the tomato sauce and place it on the cardboard circle in the pizza pan. Add toppings and point out that the recipe says it has to bake for 20 minutes. Ask if anyone knows how they will know when 20 minutes is up. Show children the timer and demonstrate how to set it for 20 minutes, naming the two numbers that make up the numeral 20. Place the pizza in the oven and gather everyone in the story corner.

Step 9　Focus children's attention on the cover of the book that you have chosen to read from the center book list (page 40). Read the title and the name of the author. Then, read the story aloud and relate the events in the story to the Pizza Restaurant. Encourage children to suggest names for the Pizza Restaurant. List their suggestions on a piece of chart paper. Let children vote on their favorite name. Tell them when the center will be open (show them the Open/Closed sign and the Hours of Operation sign). Remind them of the established rules and procedures that they followed last month when they played in the Grocery Store.

Step 10　Before opening the Pizza Restaurant to children, invite them back to the center and review the names of the props and materials. Select two children to be customers and model how to greet and seat them and take their orders. Show them the rebus menu. Ask if anyone knows what letter they see at the beginning of the word **menu** and help them to identify it, make the **M** sound and relate the sound to children's names and words that they know that begin with the same sound. Place the word card for **menu** on the word wall and write up a sample order. Select two other children to be the chefs and give them the order. Demonstrate how customers will pay the bill and show children how to use the cash register and count the money.

HINT: Limit the use of play money to one-dollar bills and pennies so it will be easier for children to count.

Demonstrate how to carry the pizza to the customers on the tray. Show children the empty cups and the straws for **sodas**. Ask children to identify the sound that they hear at the beginning of the words **soda** and **straw**. Add the word cards for **soda** and **straw** to the word wall.

Step 11　Gather the assessment materials that will be used in this center and place them in a convenient location near the Housekeeping center. In addition to the Book-Handling Checklist (page 135), the Oral Language Rating Scale (page 136), and the Socialization Skills Rating Scale (page 137), other assessment materials that may be used in this center include: the Alphabet Knowledge Assessment checklist on page 138 (letters include B, F, L, P, T, S, M), and the Shape Recognition Checklist for circle and triangle (page 139).

Fast-Food Restaurant

Goals and Objectives for Children

1. To develop an understanding of how a fast-food restaurant operates through practice and simulation

2. To develop oral communication skills through role-playing various roles, such as cashier, store manager, cook, and customer

3. To develop oral communication skills by greeting customers and taking orders

4. To develop concepts of print by reading food bags, product containers, and the center books (page 46)

5. To develop book-handling skills by reading the various books at the center

6. To develop phonemic awareness of the **K** sound in **ketchup**, the **H** sound in **hamburger**, and the **E** sound in **exit**. To reinforce previously introduced sounds including the **F** sound in **french fries**, the **P** sound in **pickle**, and the **M** sound in **mustard**

7. To develop the concept of rhyming words

8. To develop reading skills by reading environmental print and rebus menus

9. To develop writing skills by writing customers' orders and creating name tags

10. To develop math skills by counting out the correct number of items ordered by the customer, setting the timer to the number 5, and counting money

11. To develop the ability to recognize the quarter (25 cents)

12. To develop the ability to distinguish between healthy and unhealthy foods

13. To develop cooperative learning skills by interacting with other children at the Fast-Food Restaurant

Props

- Table and chairs
- Paper bags, napkins, paper cups, straws, food boxes, and french fry containers
- Spatulas for flipping burgers, tongs for stirring fries
- Play milk shake machine
- Play drink machine
- Counter area
- Cash register
- Play money
- Chef's hat and apron
- Skillet
- Plastic hamburger and chicken patties (or make them out of play dough)
- French fry basket
- Plastic french fries or fries made out of yellow strips of play dough
- Plastic trays
- Empty fruit cup containers

Print Materials

- Center sign with the name of the Fast-Food Restaurant
- Signs for Open/Closed, Exit, Hours of Operation, No Smoking
- Rebus menus
- Place mats with logos
- Order forms
- Name tags for manager, cashier, cook, customer, drink machine operator, and milk shake machine operator
- Paper with the words **hamburger**, **chicken**, **cheeseburger**, and **fruit cup** on it next to their pictures
- French fry containers with pictures of french fries and the words **french fries** clearly written on the container
- "I Like" poem written on chart paper (page 49)
- Fruit cup containers with pictures of fruit and the words **fruit cup** clearly written on the container
- Empty ketchup, mustard, salt, and pepper packages
- Rebus word cards for **K–ketchup**, **H–hamburger**, **E–exit**, **M–mustard**, **P–pickle**, **and F–french fries**
- Chart with pictures of the roles children can play in this center, including cook, french fry cook, drink maker, counter attendant, store manager, and customer
- Individual letter cards for the letters in the words **french fries**

     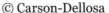

Writing Materials

- Pens and pencils

- Name tags

- Rebus order forms

- Receipts

Book List

- *The Cat Who Came for Tacos* by Diana Star Helmer (Albert Whitman and Co., 2003)
A stray cat shows up on a doorstep and is invited in for lunch. Before the cat can eat the delicious tuna tacos, he needs to learn some manners.

- *Dinner at the Panda Palace* by Stephanie Calmenson (HarperTrophy, 1995)
A variety of animals stop by to eat at the Panda Palace in this rhyming, fun-to-read-aloud book.

- *Friday Night at Hodges' Café* by Tim Egan (Houghton Mifflin, 1996)
Hodges Café is known for its delicious pastries but is selective about who can order them. After a food fight breaks out, the café decides to serve everyone.

- *Froggy Eats Out* by Jonathan London (Viking Juvenile, 2001)
Froggy goes out to dinner with his parents but has trouble dining in a fancy restaurant. Children will laugh out loud at Froggy's misadventures.

- *Miss Piggy's Night Out* by Sarah Hoagland Hunter (Puffin Books, 1995)
Miss Piggy has some problems dining in a fancy restaurant, but Kermit the Frog comes to her rescue.

Storage Container

You can use a large box decorated to resemble the fast-food restaurant that you have chosen to showcase to store all of the needed props and materials.

Implementing the Fast-Food Restaurant

Procedures:

Step 1   Visit local fast-food restaurants to decide which one will best set up in the classroom. Collect sample materials including: place mats, food containers, bags, french fry containers, fruit cups, and food boxes. Arrange to speak to the manager and tell her that you would like to use the restaurant's materials in a center in the classroom. Often, the restaurant will donate the materials. Look at the different types of literacy materials that are displayed (signs, posters, menus, name tags, etc.) so that you can create your own for the center.

Step 2   Collect or create as many props, print, and writing materials as possible from the props and materials lists. Visit the local library to check out a variety of books.

Step 3   Download appropriate environmental print, logos, food images, and signs from the Internet by accessing a search engine and typing in the name of the fast-food restaurant you have chosen. Design the place mats, rebus menus, and order slips. Write the words to the poem, "I Like" (page 49) on chart paper. Make individual letter cards for the letters in the words **french fries**.

Step 4   Choose an area close to the Housekeeping center in the classroom to set up the Fast-Food Restaurant so that children will have access to the stove. Hang the restaurant sign and display the posters and large rebus menu. Put the place mats on the table and hang up the aprons and chef's hats near the stove. Set up the milk shake maker, the french fry station, and skillets to cook the burgers and chicken (or other food served by your Fast-Food restaurant).

Step 5   Introduce the center by gathering children together close to the area where the Fast-Food Restaurant has been set up. Point out the fast-food restaurant sign and direct children to raise their hands if they have ever eaten at _____ (insert the name of your chosen restaurant). Allow time for children to share their experiences at the restaurant. Invite them to discuss their favorite foods from the restaurant. As soon as someone says, "I like hamburgers," stop and sound out the word **hamburger**. Stress the beginning **H** sound and show children the hamburgers, skillets, and spatulas that they will be using in this center. Show children the paper wrapper that has the word **hamburger** printed on it and tell them that it will be used to wrap the hamburgers. Then, show children the rebus word card for **hamburger**. Invite them to say the word aloud and compliment them on reading such a big word! Place the word card on the word wall.

Ask children what they like on their hamburgers and when someone mentions **ketchup**, show them the packages of **ketchup** and point out the word **ketchup**. Help children name the beginning letter and sound for the word **ketchup** (**K**). Show children the rebus word card for **ketchup**. Invite them to read the word again and ask for a volunteer to put the word in its correct place on the word wall. Continue asking children what they like on their hamburgers. When someone says **mustard**, repeat the same process to reinforce the **M** sound that they learned from **menu** in the Pizza Restaurant. Show children the rebus word card for **mustard**. Continue asking children what they like on their hamburgers. When someone says **pickles**, reinforce the **P** sound that is heard in the word **pickles**. Ask children if they can remember other words that start with the **P** sound. Encourage them to look at the word wall for ideas. They should recognize the words **pizza** and **pepperoni**. Reinforce the beginning sounds of children's names that begin with **P**. Add the word card for **pickle** to the word wall.

Ask children if they order anything else to go with their hamburgers. As soon as someone says **french fries**, show them the play dough or plastic french fries that they will be serving in the restaurant. Then, show children the word card for **french fries**. Help them sound out the beginning letters in **french** and **fries** and invite them to locate other words on the word wall that begin with **F**. Be sure to talk about children's names that begin with **F**. Show them the french fry basket and tongs that they will be using to make the **french fries** in the restaurant. Tell children that they can choose to have a fruit cup instead of french fries with their meals. Ask them why a fruit cup would be a healthier choice. Show them the empty fruit cup containers that they can use in this center. Point out that the word **fruit** in **fruit cup** starts with the same sound as **french fries**.

Step 6   Invite children into the Fast-Food Restaurant and show them the cooking area for the hamburgers and chicken with the skillet and spatulas, the french fry station with the fry basket and tongs, and the drinks area with the plastic cups and straws. Explain that this is where the cooks will work. Show them the name tags for the cooks and model how to cook a burger, chicken patty, and french fries. Bring out the timer and show children how to set it for five minutes. This is how long the french fries need to cook. Model how to wrap the burger in the special wrapping paper and put the chicken in a cardboard container. Demonstrate how to place the fries into the fry container and place the finished food on a tray.

 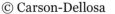

Then, show children the area where the cashiers will take the customers' orders. Invite a child to place her order by reading the large posted rebus menu and model how to record it on the preprinted rebus order pads. Point out that the little box in front of the picture is where they write the number of hamburgers, chicken patties, french fries, fruit cups, and drinks that the customer wants. You can either use tally marks or write the actual number. Model how to ring up the order on the cash register, count the customer's money, and give the order to the cooks. Prepare the customer's drink order and place the food items on a tray or in a bag when she is ready. Invite the child to enjoy her lunch! Turn the sign so it says, Closed.

Fast-Food Restaurant Order Pad

☐ hamburger

☐ chicken sandwich

☐ french fries

☐ fruit cup

☐ drink(s)

Step 7   Gather children into the reading area and show them the chart-paper poem "I Like." Read the poem aloud, line by line, tracking the print with your finger or a pointer. Read the poem again, inviting children to read it aloud.

I Like

I like to go out to eat,

I order french fries and meat.

Show them the **french fries** word card from the word wall and ask someone to find it on the chart. Invite children to tell how they knew that the letters on the chart spell **french fries**. Point out the beginning letters of each word and ask children to name the beginning letter and make its sound. Use individual letter cards for the letters in french fries so children can match them to the printed letters of the chart paper poem. Children can do this activity now and later when they play in the Fast-Food Restaurant.

Then, track the word **eat** and the word **meat** in the poem with your hand. Ask children to say the two words and listen carefully to hear how they sound alike. Tell them that words that sound alike are rhyming words. Have children repeat the words again. If they are familiar with rhyming words, say some other pairs of words and ask them if they rhyme. If rhyming is a new concept to children in your class, you may want to wait before reviewing additional rhyming words.

Choose a book from the center book list (page 46). Show children the cover of the book that you will read aloud. Read the title and the author and invite children to make predictions about the story based on the cover and the title. Take a picture walk through the story, pointing out things that are similar to what is in their restaurant. Read the story aloud, and then go back and check children's predictions. Tell them that tomorrow they will get to act out parts of the story when they play in the restaurant. Show them the other books that they can look at while they play in the Fast-Food Restaurant.

Step 8   Before opening the Fast-Food Restaurant to children, invite them back into the center and review the various roles that they can play in this center. Assign a volunteer to be the cook, the french fry cooker, the drink maker, the cashier, the customer, and the store manager. Ask a child to place his order so everyone can act out their roles. Give the participants their name tags and tell them to write their names. Provide name cards for children to copy from if necessary, or direct them to use the name chart. Invite children without roles to watch carefully and make sure that everyone does their jobs correctly. Allow time for children to act out placing, preparing, and serving an order. Inform children that when they play the role of the customer, they can look at the books in the center while waiting for their order.

Step 9   Gather children together, and before opening the Fast-Food Restaurant, review the rules that have been posted in the classroom. Show children the chart and name the various roles that they can play. Tell them that the customer does not need a name tag and ask them why. Tell them how many children can play in the center at one time and remind them that this center will be up for three to four weeks so that everyone will have the chance to play in the restaurant. Review all of the words that have been introduced in this center.

Step 10 Gather the assessment materials that will be used in the Fast-Food Restaurant and place them in a convenient location near the center. You will use the Book-Handling Checklist (page 135), the Oral Language Rating Scale (page 136), the Shape Recognition Assessment (page 139), and the Number Recognition Assessment (page 140).

 # Doctor's Office

Goals and Objectives for Children

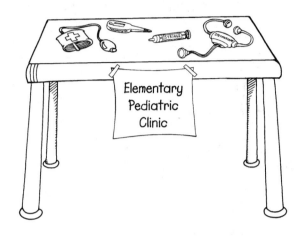

1. To develop an understanding of how a doctor's office operates through practice and simulation

2. To develop oral communication skills through role-playing various roles, such as doctor, nurse, receptionist, physician's assistant, and patient

3. To develop oral communication skills by greeting patients, talking with patients, explaining why a patient is not feeling well, and describing how to get better

4. To develop concepts of print by reading pamphlets, eye charts, patient charts, and the center books (page 53)

5. To reinforce book-handling skills by encouraging children to read the various books at the center, especially nonfiction books

6. To develop phonemic awareness and letter recognition of the **D** sound in **doctor**, the **N** sound in **nurse**, the **C** sound in **cold**, the **I** sound in **itchy** and **in**, the **Q** sound in **Q-Tips®**, and the **X** sound in **X-ray** and reinforce the **F** sound in **flu**, the **H** sound in **hurt** and **healthy**, the **P** sound in **patient**, and the **S** sound in **sick**

7. To reinforce an awareness of rhyming words

8. To develop reading skills by reading environmental print and patient charts

9. To introduce nonfiction literature

10. To develop writing skills by filling out patient charts, writing prescriptions, creating name tags, recording patient appointment times in the appointment book, and by completing cards for future appointments

11. To develop math skills by practicing reading numbers on thermometers, scales, and counting out "pills"

12. To develop cooperative learning skills by interacting with other children at the Doctor's Office

13. To develop nonstereotypical concepts of gender in the workplace

     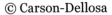

Props

- Doctor's bag
- Stethoscope
- Thermometer
- Plastic syringe
- Telephone
- Lab coats
- Rubber gloves
- Tongue depressors
- Sterile masks
- Scales
- Blood pressure gauge
- Elastic bandages

- Empty prescription bottles
- Tape
- Adhesive bandages
- Play money
- Play debit/credit cards
- Gauze
- Cot
- Table
- Bingo chips for pills
- X-rays
- Cotton swabs
- Dolls

Print Materials

- Center sign with the name of the Doctor's Office
- Calendar
- Eye chart
- Rebus symptom checklist
- Environmental print insurance cards
- Folders and charts for patients
- Literature and pamphlets
- Magazines for waiting area
- Signs for Open/Closed, Exit, Hours of Operation, No Smoking, Check In Here, Check Out Here, Exam Room

- Name tags
- Rebus word cards for **D–doctor**, **N–nurse**, **C–cold**, **I–itchy**, **I–in**, **H–hurt**, **H–healthy**, **P–patient**, **and S–sick**
- Chart with pictures of the roles children can play in this center, including doctor, nurse, receptionist, physician's assistant, and patient
- "Sick, Sick, Sick" poem written on chart paper (page 54)
- Rhyming words from "Sick, Sick, Sick" copied onto index cards

Writing Materials

- Patient sign-in book
- Appointment book
- Pens and pencils
- Prescription pads
- Patient charts
- Appointment cards

- Insurance forms
- Rebus symptom checklist
- Office visit billing statement
- Bills/receipts/charge slips
- Folders
- Labels for the doctor's tools

Book List

- *The Berenstain Bears Go to the Doctor* by Stan and Jan Berenstain (Random House Books for Young Readers, 1981)
  Brother and Sister Bear have to go to the doctor for a checkup.

- *Corduroy Goes to the Doctor* by Don Freeman (Viking Juvenile, 1987)
  Children will learn all about Corduroy's physical exam at the doctor's office.

- *A Day in the Life of a Doctor* by Linda Hayward (DK Children, 2001)
  This nonfiction book shows the tools doctors use as they go through their daily routine of treating patients.

- *Doctor Maisy* by Lucy Cousins (Candlewick Press, 2001)
  Maisy puts on a white doctor coat and treats a panda with a thermometer and a stethoscope.

- *Doctor Tools* by Inez Synder (Children's Press, 2002)
  Maya goes to the doctor and introduces the reader to the various tools that a doctor uses while treating a patient.

- *Froggy Goes to the Doctor* by Jonathan London (Viking Children's Books, 2002)
  All kinds of funny events occur when Froggy goes to see Dr. Mugwort.

Storage Container

A large canvas bag with a large red cross on it can be used to store all of the needed props and supplies. A smaller canvas bag with handles or a black purse with a red cross on it can be used as a doctor bag.

     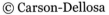

Implementing the Doctor's Office

Procedures:

Step 1   Visit a local doctor's office or clinic to collect pamphlets and other literature. Observe the surroundings carefully to see how the office and waiting room are set up and note what kinds of literacy materials (signs, charts, etc.) are displayed. Observe the office procedures to see how patients sign in and out, how they are called for their appointments, and how they check out. Ask office personnel if they have any samples, old X-rays, or other free props or materials.

Step 2   Collect or create as many of the props, print, and writing materials as possible from the props and materials lists. Visit the library to check out a variety of fiction and nonfiction books.

Step 3   Design the large canvas bag and the small doctor bag (page 53). Download appropriate environmental print and signs from the Internet by accessing a search engine and typing in the keywords **doctor's office** and **signs**. Create a rebus symptom checklist, insurance forms, billing statements, patient folders, patient charts, name tags, charge slips, appointment book, sign-in pad, and the rest of the writing materials by incorporating the downloaded images into the various forms. Copy the poem "Sick, Sick, Sick" onto chart paper. Remember to leave enough space between the lines so children can match the words.

Step 4   Choose an area in the classroom and set up the cot or long table that will be used for the patient's bed. If possible, hang a blanket from the ceiling to the floor that will separate the bed from the waiting room, or use bookcases to divide the space. Arrange two to three chairs in the waiting area and display the magazines, doctor books, and pamphlets. Use a table or small desk to serve as the reception area. Hang all of the signs, label the props, arrange the materials for the reception area, and display the doctor's coat and bag.

Step 5   Introduce the center by gathering children together in the reading corner in front of the chart-paper poem "Sick, Sick, Sick." Read the entire poem to children, tracking the print with your hand or a pointer. Then, have them repeat the poem line by line. Read it again and add hand motions. (After the first line, place a hand on your forehead and grimace. After the second line, beckon with

> Sick, Sick, Sick
> I woke up feeling sick, sick, sick,
> I called for my mommy to come quick, quick, quick!
> My mommy called for the doctor right away
> And the doctor said she'd come today.
> She gave me some pills, pills, pills
> And a lot of bills, bills, bills.

 54   © Carson-Dellosa   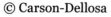   CD-104231 • Literacy Play Centers

your finger. After the third line, pretend to push the buttons on a phone. After the fourth line, nod your head. After the fifth line, pretend to pass out pills. After the final line, pretend to pass out pieces of paper.)

Point out the rhyming words in the poem. Have children repeat the rhyming words. Show them the word card for **sick** and place it on the word wall. Print each of the rhyming words on cards so children can match them to the words on the chart.

Step 6 Direct children to raise their hands if they have ever been to a doctor's office. Place the doctor's bag where children can see it and generate a discussion about going to the doctor's office. Begin the discussion by asking, "What happens at the doctor's office?" If a child mentions getting his temperature taken, open the doctor's bag and take out the thermometer. You may want to construct a thermometer out of poster board with a piece of white elastic

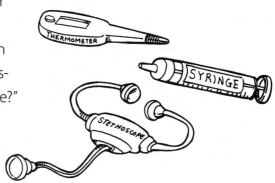

(to represent a normal temperature). Color part of the elastic red (to represent a fever). Model how to take someone's temperature using a doll and show students how to read the numbers on the thermometer. If a child mentions that the doctor listened to her heart, show children the stethoscope and demonstrate how to use it. Each time children mention a procedure, pull out the appropriate item from the bag and model how to use it. Point out that each instrument has been labeled with its name.

Tell children that they will have a chance to be a doctor in their new center, the Doctor's Office. Point to the Doctor's Office sign that is hanging at the center. Show them the rebus word card for **doctor** (page 52). Point to the pictures (male and female) and the word **doctor** and direct children to read it aloud. Ask children how many of them have a doctor who is a woman and how many have a doctor who is a man. Stress the beginning **D** sound and ask children to name the beginning letter of **doctor**. Ask for a volunteer to place the word card for **doctor** in its appropriate place on the word wall. Ask children if they know what to call the person who helps the doctor. Show them the rebus word card for **nurse**. Point to the pictures (male and female) and the word **nurse**. Ask if anyone has ever had a male nurse. Point to the beginning letter (**N**) and have children name it and make that sound. Ask for another volunteer to place the word card for **nurse** on the word wall. Then, ask children if they know what you call someone who needs to be seen by a doctor. Lead them to say **patient**. Accent the beginning sound and name the letter (**P**). Ask children to recall what center they played in before that began with the **P** sound (Pizza Restaurant). Show them the word card for **patient** and add it to the word wall. Take this opportunity to read all of the **P** words on the word wall.

Ask children why they have had to go to the doctor's office. If someone says she had the flu, show children the word card for **flu**. Point out the beginning letter and ask children to name other words that begin with the **F** sound. Place the word card for **flu** in the F section of the word wall and read all of the **F** words on the word wall. Tell children that you went to the doctor's office once when you had a really bad cold. Show them the rebus word card for **cold** and ask them to identify the beginning letter and make the sound that **C** makes. Ask a volunteer to place the word card for **cold** on the word wall. Tell children the doctor sees lots of people who have rashes and are **itchy**. Have them repeat the word **itchy** and model how to make the **I** sound. Show children the word card with **itchy** on it and ask them to name the beginning letter. Ask them to show where the word itchy belongs on the word wall. Then, choose a volunteer to place it on the word wall.

Ask children if they have ever had an earache. Tell them how important it is to keep their ears clean. Show children a **Q-tips**® cotton swab and ask if their parents have ever cleaned their ears with one. Show the word card for **Q-tip** and ask a volunteer to place it on the word wall. Model how to clean a doll's ears with a **Q-tip** and stress that the **Q-tips**® cotton swabs can only be used with the dolls.

Tell children that it is important for them to stay healthy and not get hurt. Show them the word cards for **healthy** and **hurt** and have them name the beginning letter. Model how to feel air blowing on your hand when you make the **H** sound. Add the word cards for **healthy** and **hurt** to the word wall.

Ask children if they have ever had any broken bones. Ask how the doctor knew that the bone was broken. Show them a picture of an **X-ray** (or an actual X-ray, if possible) and allow time for them to look at it carefully. Then, invite children to read the word **X-ray** on the word card and place it on the word wall.

Step 7   Gather children in the reading area and show them the book, *Doctor's Tools* by Inez Synder (Children's Press, 2002) or another nonfiction book about doctors. Show children the cover of the book and read the title and author. Ask them to describe what they see on the front cover. Tell children that this book is different from other stories you have read to them because it contains facts and is called nonfiction. Ask children to predict what kinds of tools they think will be described in the book. Be sure to have the doctor's kit close by so that you can show the tools as they are discussed in the story. Read the story aloud and invite children to repeat the names of the doctor's tools.

Step 8   Show children the chart with the roles that they can play at this center. Take them into the center and point out the waiting room with the books, magazines, and other literature they can read while waiting for the receptionist to call their names. Show them where the receptionist will sit and model how to check in with the receptionist and sign the check-in book. Point to the Check In sign and ask them to guess what it says. Show them the Doctor Is In sign and the word card for **in**. Have children match the word card to the word **in** on the signs. Add the word card for **in** to the word wall. Then, take them into the exam room and show them the cot where patients lie down so the doctor can examine them. Ask a volunteer to be the patient. Put on the doctor's coat and surgical mask and model how to treat a patient. Ask the patient to spell her name so that you can write it on the folder and on the rebus symptom checklist. Then, ask the child to describe what hurts. Model how to check off symptoms on the checklist. Demonstrate how to examine the patient using all of the tools in the doctor's bag. Share your diagnosis with the patient. Model how to write a prescription on the prescription pad and give the patient a medicine bottle. Tell the patient to schedule another appointment with the receptionist because she will need to come back in two weeks. Lead children back to the waiting room and assume the role of the receptionist. Fill out a billing statement and an insurance form. Ask the patient whether she will pay cash or charge the office visit. Give the patient a receipt and schedule the next appointment. Model how to fill out an appointment card and hand it to the patient. Tell children that the Doctor's Office is now closed and turn the sign to Closed.

Step 9   Prior to opening the Doctor's Office for children to play in, review the rules that are posted in the classroom. Tell them how many children can play in this center at one time and remind them that the Doctor's Office will be open for three to four weeks so that everyone will have a chance to play there. Review all of the word cards for this center.

Step 10   Gather the assessment materials that will be used in the Doctor's Office and place them in a convenient location near the center. The assessment instruments include the Socialization Skills Rating Scale (page 137), Alphabet Knowledge Assessment (page 138), Number Recognition Assessment (page 140), and Emergent and Early Writing Rubric (page 141). (Check to see if children recognize all of the letters that have been introduced so far in the four literacy play centers. Letters include B, F, L, P, M, T, S, K, H, E, D, N, C, I, X, and Q.)

Shoe Store

Goals and Objectives for Children

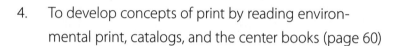

1. To develop an understanding of how a shoe store operates through practice and simulation

2. To develop oral communication skills through role-playing various roles, such as store clerk, store manager, cashier, stock boy or girl, and customer

3. To develop oral communication skills by greeting customers and engaging in conversations about shoes

4. To develop concepts of print by reading environmental print, catalogs, and the center books (page 60)

5. To reinforce book-handling skills by encouraging children to read catalogs and the various books in the center

6. To develop phonemic awareness and letter recognition of the **O** sound in **open**, the **V** sound in **Velcro®**, and to reinforce the **C** sound in **clerk**, **N** sound in **newspaper**, **P** sound in **purse**, **S** sound in **shoes, sandals, socks**, and **sneakers**, the **B** sound in **boots**, and the **Q** sound in **question mark**

7. To develop reading skills by reading shoe boxes and environmental print and identifying question marks

8. To develop writing skills by filling out customers' bills, creating name tags and price tags for shoes, and using question marks

9. To develop math skills by measuring feet, sizing shoes, reading the numbers on rulers, counting money, and recognizing rectangles

10. To develop math skills by matching, classifying, and graphing pairs of shoes and socks

11. To develop estimation skills by guessing which type of shoes appears the most and least

12. To develop cooperative learning skills by interacting with other children in the shoe store

13. To develop color recognition by placing orders for different-color shoes

14. To develop fine-motor skills by lacing, tying, and buckling shoes

Props

- Sandals, tennis shoes, high heels, boots, flip-flops, and other kinds of shoes
- Shoelaces and a lacing board
- Pairs of socks
- Purses
- Shoe polish
- Cash register
- Play money
- Counter area

- Variety of different-sized shoeboxes
- Telephone
- Cardboard shoe patterns with rulers glued on them
- Small stool
- Two tables for shoe displays
- Four plastic hoops
- Pieces of paper or self-stick notes in four different colors

Print Materials

- Center sign with the name of the Shoe Store
- Newspaper ads of shoes
- Shoe catalogs
- Signs for Open/Closed, Exit, Hours of Operation, Sale, Clearance
- Labels and pictures for classifying types of shoes: shoes with laces, shoes with Velcro®, shoes with buckles, and slip-on shoes
- A graph made on a large piece of paper for children to classify their shoes

- Receipts for shoe sales
- A chart with pictures of the roles children can play in this center, including store clerk, store manager, cashier, stock clerk, and customer
- Rebus word cards for **O–open**, **V–Velcro®**, **C–clerk**, **N–newspaper**, **P–purse**, **S–shoes**, **S–sandals**, **S–sneakers**, **S–socks**, and **Q–question mark**
- Department store catalogs
- "Shoes" poem written on chart paper (page 64)

Writing Materials

- Name tags
- Bills/receipts/charge slips
- Checks
- Paper to create sale ads
- Order forms

Book List

- *Fox in Socks* by Dr. Seuss (Random House Books for Young Readers, 1965)
  This is a rhyming, nonsense book that is fun to read.

- *How Big Is a Foot?* by Rolf Myller (Yearling Books, 1991)
  Children will understand how big a foot is and will be introduced to the concept of using feet to measure distances.

- *A Pair of Red Clogs* by Masako Matsuno (Purple House Press, 2002)
  This fiction book tells the story of a little Japanese girl who loves her shiny red clogs.

- *Red Lace, Yellow Lace: Learn to Tie Your Shoe* by Mark Casey and Judith Herbst (Barron's Educational Series, 1996)
  Children will learn how to tie their shoes with the help of step-by-step illustrations and a model shoe with real laces.

- *Shoes* by Elizabeth Winthrop (HarperFestival, 1996)
  This rhyming book introduces children to a variety of shoes.

- *Shoes, Shoes, Shoes* by Ann Morris (HarperTrophy, 1998)
  This multicultural book uses colorful photographs to teach children about all kinds of shoes worn in different countries.

- *Smelly Socks* by Robert Munsch (Cartwheel, 2005)
  Tina loves her brand-new socks so much that she doesn't want to take them off. Her socks get so smelly that her friends have to find a way to make her take them off.

- *Things That Are the Most in the World* by Judi Barrett (Aladdin, 2001)
  This book teaches children the concept of most.

- *Tie Your Shoes: Rocket Style/Bunny Ears* by Leslie Bockol (Innovative Kids, 2003)
  Children will learn two different ways of tying their shoes in this fun board book.

Storage Container

A large box decorated with pictures of shoes and purses can be used to store all of the needed props and materials.

Implementing the Shoe Store

Procedures:

Step 1   Visit local shoe stores to see how they are set up and to ask for empty shoe boxes. Notice the types of displays and other examples of environmental print.

Step 2   Collect as many shoe boxes and pairs of shoes as possible. Send a letter home to parents asking them to send in shoe boxes and old pairs of shoes. (Be sure to spray all of the shoes with disinfectant.) Decide if socks will be included in this center, and if so, acquire a collection. Visit a local library to check out books. Collect shoe ads, shoe catalogs, and department store catalogs.

Step 3   Download appropriate environmental print, logos, and signs from the Internet. Reuse signs from other centers if appropriate. Add price tags to the shoe boxes. Cut foot shapes out of poster board and attach rulers to them to measure children's feet. Write the poem "Shoes" (page 64) on chart paper. Remember to leave space between the lines of the poem so that children will have room to match the words.

Step 4   Choose an area in the classroom with shelves that can accommodate the shoe boxes. Arrange the boxes on the shelves, set up the counter area, and hang the signs. Create a chart of the roles that children can play in this center by placing images of a store manager, stock person, customers, salesperson, and cashier. Attach an envelope with blank name tags next to each character. Children can write their names on these, or they may use the preprinted name tags.

Step 5   Prior to introducing the Shoe Store to children, tell them to take off their shoes. Place four large plastic hoops on the floor. Label the first hoop Shoes with Shoelaces, the second hoop Shoes with Velcro®, the third hoop Shoes with Buckles, and the fourth hoop Shoes that Slip On. (Include a picture of each type of shoe next to the label.) Ask each child to classify her shoes by placing one shoe in the correct hoop. Model this procedure by placing one of your shoes in the correct hoop. After all of the shoes have been placed in the correct hoops, ask children to predict which hoop has the most shoes, and which hoop has the least shoes. Ask children how they can find out which hoop has the most shoes. Lead them to discover that they can count the shoes. Count the shoes with children to discover if their predictions were correct. Record the total numbers for each type of shoe. Direct children to sit around the hoop that contains their shoe. Give each child a piece of colorful paper that matches her shoe type (for example, shoes with laces get blue, shoes with Velcro® get red, shoes with buckles get yellow, and slip-on shoes get green). Then, show children the large paper graph (page 62) and direct them to place their colorful paper in the matching column on the graph. Once again, model how to do this with your colorful paper. After children have attached their colorful pieces of paper, encourage them to read the results. Point out how easy it is to discover which type of shoe has the most by just looking at how tall each column is. Tell children that they have just made a graph. Ask for a volunteer to point to the type of shoe that has the most colorful pieces of paper. Count the paper pieces and record the number. Check to be sure that this number matches the number that they had counted earlier for that type of shoe. Repeat this procedure for the type of shoes that had the least number of colorful pieces of paper. If two columns have the same amount of colorful pieces of paper, seize this opportunity to introduce the term **equal**. Count and record the total number of colorful pieces of paper for the remaining types of shoes. Then, have children find their shoes and put them back on. Observe to see who can tie and/or buckle their own shoes. Tell children that they will have the opportunity to sell shoes in their new literacy play center, the Shoe Store. You may want to have children classify their shoes by color, predict, and graph the results on another day.

Shoes with Laces	Shoes with Buckles	Slip-On Shoes

Step 6   Introduce this center by gathering children together in front of the Shoe Store sign. Show them the word card for **shoes** and point out that shoes begins and ends with the same letter. Ask children to name the letter (**S**) and find it on the word wall. Ask a volunteer to add the word card for **shoes** to the word wall. Then, show children all of the shoe boxes on the shelves and tell them that the boxes are empty and that their job is to fill them with shoes. Dump out all of the shoes that have been placed in a large bag and ask children to help figure out how to stock the shelves. Explain that people called stock clerks are responsible for keeping the shelves full of shoes. Help children figure out that they need to match the shoes. Explain that shoes are sold in pairs and ask them why they think shoes are sold in pairs (a pair of feet needs a pair of shoes). Ask volunteers to match the shoes by color and size. Then, explain that each pair of shoes needs a shoe box. Show children three different-sized shoe boxes and ask if anyone knows what to call the shape of a shoe box. Show them the lids and trace the long and short sides and count the number of sides. Stress that rectangles normally have two short sides and two long sides. Show children the word card for **rectangle** and ask them to say the word aloud. Stress the beginning sound (**R**), point out how long this word is, and ask a volunteer to place the word on the

 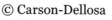

word wall. Then, model how to match large shoes to large shoe boxes and small shoes to small shoe boxes. Match as many pairs of shoes as possible to shoe boxes. Tell children that small sizes should go on the top shelf, medium sizes should go on the middle shelf, and large sizes should be placed on the bottom shelf. Ask volunteers to be stock clerks and place the shoes on the shelves. Introduce the word card for **clerk**, point out the beginning letter (**C**), and have children read the word aloud. Ask a different volunteer to place the word card for **clerk** on the word wall.

Show children the Sale sign and tell them that shoe stores often select shoes to be on sale for a reduced price. Ask children to select some of the leftover shoes to place on the sale table. Show them the newspaper ad for shoes that you created and model how to read it. Identify the **sneakers** and the **sandals** from the ad and show children the word cards for **sneakers** and **sandals**. Ask volunteers to read the words and place them on the word wall. Tell children that customers read the ads in the paper to find out what shoes are on sale. Then, show them the Clearance sign and explain that shoe stores often select some shoes to sell for a lot less money. Place the remainder of the shoes on the clearance table.

Randomly pass out the **socks** to children and invite them to describe the socks' colors and designs. Then, direct them to find the person who has a matching sock. Sort the socks by color and pattern, and place them on display. Show children the word card for **socks** and have a volunteer place it on the word wall.

Hold up a **purse** and tell children that shoe stores often sell a variety of purses. Ask children what letter they hear at the beginning of the word **purse**. Stress the **P** sound and direct children to read the word **purse**. Ask a volunteer to place the word card for **purse** on the word wall.

Step 7   During story time, share a story from the center book list (page 60). Remind children that they will be able to play in the Shoe Store soon. Then, share the chart paper poem, "Shoes" (page 64). Point out the word **shoes** and have children count how many times the word **shoes** appears in this poem. Show the word card for **shoes** and ask a volunteer to match it to the word **shoes** in the poem. Ask children to identify the beginning and ending letter. Then, point out the **question mark** and ask children if they have ever seen this mark before. Explain to them that

     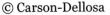

this mark is used whenever a writer is asking a question. You may want to use this opportunity to have children practice identifying questions by saying simple statements and instructing children to raise their hands whenever they hear a question. Show them the word card for **question mark**, stress the beginning sound, and ask a volunteer to add it to the word wall.

> **Shoes**
>
> Red shoes, blue shoes,
>
> Black shoes, brown shoes,
>
> Shoes with laces, shoes that tie,
>
> Oh, which pair should I buy?

Step 8   Before opening the Shoe Store to children, invite them back to the store and review the types of shoes and the other props. Select two children to be customers and model how to introduce yourself to them by pointing to your name tag. Demonstrate how to ask customers what kind of shoes they are looking to buy. Lead customers around the center, pointing out the shoes that are on sale, as well as the shoes on the clearance table. After the customers select their shoes, model how to measure their feet with the feet patterns. Find the shoes that customers want and show how to fit them on customers' feet. Ask customers if they would like to buy some extra shoelaces or polish for their new shoes. Also, ask customers if they would like to buy a purse to match their shoes. (Point out to children that you are asking questions.) Model how to write the bill and walk the customers to the cash register to take their money and write a receipt.

Step 9   Prior to opening the Shoe Store for children to play in, review the rules that are posted in the classroom. Tell them how many children can play in this center at one time and remind them that the Shoe Store will be open for three to four weeks so that everyone will have a chance to play there.

Step 10 Review all of the word cards for this center. Show children the various books that have been placed in the center and encourage them to read these books while this center is open. Show them the Open sign and ask them to read the word **open** with you. Stress the beginning sound and demonstrate how the mouth forms an **O** shape when saying the **O** sound. Add the word card for **open** to the word wall.

Step 11 Gather the assessment materials that will be used for this center. You will need the Book-Handling Checklist (page 135), the Oral language Rating Scale (page 136), and the Socialization Skills Rating Scale (page 137).

 # Veterinary Office

Goals and Objectives for Children

Preschool Veterinary Clinic

1. To develop an understanding of how a veterinary office operates through practice and simulation

2. To develop oral communication skills through role-playing various roles, such as veterinarian (vet), a pet owner, a nurse, and a receptionist

3. To develop concepts of print by reading pamphlets, charts, center books (page 67), and other printed materials

4. To reinforce book-handling skills by encouraging children to read the various books at the center

5. To develop phonemic awareness and letter recognition of the **A** sound in **animal**, and to reinforce the **B** sound in **bird**, the **C** sound in **cat**, the **D** sound in **dog**, the **P** sound in **pet**, and the **V** sound in **veterinary** and **vet**

6. To reinforce an awareness of rhyming words

7. To develop reading skills by reading environmental print, labels and signs, and by interpreting classmates' writing

8. To develop writing skills by filling out prescriptions, charts, and creating notes for patients

9. To develop math skills by measuring and reading numbers on thermometers and scales

10. To develop one-to-one correspondence by placing each pet in its own cage

11. To develop cooperative learning skills by interacting with other children at the Veterinary Office

    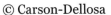

Props

- Doctor's bag
- Stethoscope
- Thermometer
- Plastic syringe
- Telephone
- Lab coats
- Stuffed animals
- Plastic bins for cages
- Rubber gloves
- Tongue depressor
- Sterile masks

- Gauze
- Elastic bandages
- Scales
- Blood pressure gauge
- Empty medicine bottles
- Tape
- Adhesive bandages
- Play money
- Play checks
- Play debit/credit cards
- Money tray

Print Materials

- Center sign with name of the Veterinary Office
- Calendar
- Pet literature
- Signs for Open/Closed, Exit, Hours of Operation, Exam Room, No Smoking
- Charts
- Rebus symptom checklist
- Environmental print insurance cards
- Folders for patients

- Magazines for waiting area
- Folder
- Pet/Animal chart
- Rebus word cards for **A–animal**, **B–bird**, **C–cat**, **D–dog**, **P–pet**, **V–vet**
- Chart with pictures of the roles children can play in this center including vet, pet owner, nurse, and receptionist
- "I Had a Little Pet" (page 69) written on chart paper

Writing Materials

- Sign-in book
- Appointment book
- Pens and pencils
- Name tags
- Prescription pad

- Rebus pet diagnosis sheet
- Office visit billing statement
- Checks
- Bills/receipts/charge slips
- Folders

Book List

- *Arthur's Pet Business* by Marc Brown (Little, Brown and Co., 1993)
  Arthur learns how to be responsible for taking care of a pet so his parents will buy him a puppy.

- *Biscuit* by Alyssa Satin Capucilli (HarperTrophy, 1997)
  Biscuit is a small yellow puppy who has his own bedtime routine.

- *Clifford the Big Red Dog* by Norman Bridwell (Cartwheel, 1995)
  Emily loves to take care of her giant, red dog.

- *Curious George and the Puppies* by H. A. Rey (Houghton Mifflin, 1998)
  Curious George and the man with the yellow hat go to an animal shelter where George accidentally lets all of the dogs out of their cages.

- *Dear Mrs. LaRue: Letters from Obedience School* by Mark Teague (Scholastic Press, 2002)
  Ike's owner has sent him away to a school for bad dogs. Find out his exciting plan to get home.

- *A Fish Out of Water* by Helen Palmer (Random House Books for Young Readers, 1961)
  A little boy buys a fish at the pet store but overfeeds him and the fish grows and grows.

- *Have You Seen My Cat?* by Eric Carle (Aladdin, 1997)
  A young boy meets many different types of cats while searching for his lost cat.

- *Mr. Betts and Mr. Potts* by Rod Hull (Barefoot Books, 2000)
  In this rhyming story, Mr. Betts takes all of his pets to the vet.

- *Pick a Pet* by Shelley Rotner (Scholastic, 1999)
  Patty dreams about all kinds of pets that she would like to have before deciding she wants a puppy.

- *Puppy Mudge Takes a Bath* by Cynthia Rylant (Aladdin, 2004)
  Henry's puppy, Mudge, loves to play in the mud, but she hates to take a bath. So Henry joins him in the tub!

- *Sally Goes to the Vet* by Stephen Huneck (Harry N. Abrams, Inc., 2004)
  Sally, a black lab, describes her visit to the vet's office.

- *Who's Peeking at You? In the Pet Store* by Richard Powell (Barron's Educational Series, 2006)
  A puppy sees a pair of eyes and finds a kitten. Who else might the puppy find in the pet store?

    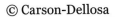

Storage Container

Use a large canvas bag with a red cross on it and attach various pictures of animals. This bag can be placed inside the largest crate or bin that will be used as a cage. Smaller bins can be nested inside the large bin. All of the other props and writing materials should fit in the canvas bag.

Implementing the Veterinary Office

Procedures:

Step 1   Visit a local veterinary office to collect pamphlets and other literature. Look carefully to see how the office and waiting room are set up and note what kind of literacy materials (signs, charts, etc.) are displayed. Observe the office procedures (how "patients" sign in and out, how pets get to the examining rooms, how pets get brought up front from the kennel, etc.). Ask for free materials.

Step 2   Collect or create as many props, print, and writing materials as possible from the props and materials lists. Visit the library to check out books. Be sure to get some fiction and nonfiction books.

Step 3   Design the storage bag (local craft stores sell a variety of canvas bags). Cut out pictures of various animals from magazines or download pictures from the Internet. Gather a variety of different-sized bins, crates, or other containers to serve as cages. Label each cage with the type of stuffed animal that will fit inside. Download appropriate environmental print and signs from the Internet. Create the rebus symptom checklist, patient charts and diagnosis sheets, name tags, billing statements and charge slips, appointment book, sign-in pad, prescription pad, and any other materials that you want to include in this center. Copy the poem "I Had a Little Pet" (page 69) on chart paper. Be sure to copy it exactly as it is written.

Step 4   Choose an area in the classroom that can be separated from the rest of the classroom. Hang the sign of the name of the Veterinary Office at children's eye level. Arrange the materials within the designated space to resemble a real vet's office.

Step 5   Introduce the center by gathering children together in a space close to the whiteboard/chalkboard. Initiate a discussion by asking children to raise their hands if they have a pet. Then, ask if their pet has ever been sick, and if so, what did they do? If the term **veterinarian** is not mentioned, tell them a pet doctor is called a **veterinarian**. Write the word on a whiteboard and point out the beginning letter by placing your hand under the beginning letter, **V**, naming the letter and saying the **V** sound. Have children repeat the letter/sound with you. Remind them

 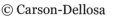

of other words that they are familiar with that also start with **V**. If you have a child whose name starts with **V**, say that name aloud, and chant the words and environmental print that begin with **V** from the word wall. Help them recall that Valentine's also starts with **V**.

Share that people often refer to the veterinarian as just the "vet". Point out the first three letters of veterinarian and underline them with a marker or with your hand. Write those three letters on the whiteboard (vet) and ask children who vets help. Guide them to say pet. Write the word **pet** under **vet** and point out how these words sound alike. Remind children that words that sound alike are called rhyming words.

Step 6   Share the finger play "I Had a Little Pet" with students.

Begin by using your hand or a pointer to underline each word in the title. Ask children to read it aloud. Ask them if there is a word in the title that they have seen before. Ask a volunteer to come to the chart and point to the word **pet**. Name the letters that spell **pet**. Show how the letters in the word **pet** recorded earlier on the whiteboard are identical to the word **pet** in the title of the finger play. Read the entire finger play again to children, pointing to each word with your hand or a pointer. Then, invite children to say the finger play again. Model enthu-siasm, correct phrasing, and stress the rhyming words. Say/read the finger play with children two to three times. Ask them if they can find the word that says **vet**. Have a volunteer point it out on the chart. Ask them if they can find a word that rhymes with **vet**. Once again, choose a volun-teer to point to the word on the chart. Then, ask children to help spell **vet** to be sure it is spelled correctly on the word card. Repeat the same procedure with the word **pet**. Invite the class to read the word cards aloud. Underline the **et** ending in **pet** and **vet** and review that those two words rhyme. Point out that only the first letter of each word is different. Ask if anyone can find other words in the finger play that rhyme. (Reread the finger play again if necessary.) Point out **sick**, **sick**, **sick** and **quick**, **quick**, **quick**. Ask them how they know that these words rhyme. Lead them to see that just like **vet** and **pet** sounded alike and ended with the same letters (**et**), **sick** and **quick** also sound alike and end with the same letters (**ick**).

This activity can be adapted by writing the word **pet** on a card and attaching it to the finger play chart with Velcro®. Next time the finger play is shared, exchange the word **pet** for a specific animal name, such as dog, cat, bird, or other animal from the animal chart.

> I Had a Little Pet
>
> I had a little pet
>
> That was sick, sick, sick
>
> I took him to the vet
>
> Quick, quick, quick!

    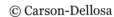

Step 7 Choose a book from the list to read aloud to children. (If a fiction book is chosen, be sure to read a nonfiction book to children before they return to play in the vet's office.) After reading, discuss the pet in the story. Remind children that pets are animals. Stress the beginning sound while pointing to the **A** in **animal**. Invite a volunteer to place this word card on the word wall.

Step 8 Ask children if they have ever taken their pet to a vet. Call on volunteers to describe what happened. Build and elaborate on their recollections. If no one has experienced a visit to the vet, describe in your own words what a visit to the vet's office is like. Use the stuffed animals in the discussion. Be sure to describe the people who work in a vet's office (put on the doctor coat and mask) and the specific procedures that a visitor would go through, from entering and signing in, to the checkup with the vet, to paying for the visit (use the props).

Step 9 Show children the Veterinary Office center. Share the rest of the props and materials that have been placed in the center. Tell them the center will be open for three to four weeks so that everyone will have a chance to play in it. Remind them of the established procedures for playing in the center. Review all of the word cards for this center.

Step 10 Gather the assessment materials that will be used with this center and place them in a convenient location near the center. Assessment materials used with this center include: Book-Handling Checklist (page 135), Socialization Skills Rating Scale (page 137), Alphabet Knowledge Assessment (page 138), Shape Recognition Checklist (page 139), and Rhyming Words (page 142). Check to see if children recognize all of the letters that have been introduced so far in the six Literacy Play Centers, including B, F, L, P, M, T, S, K, H, E, D, N, C, I, X, Q, O, V, R, and A.

Barbershop/Hair Salon

Goals and Objectives for Children

Clemmons Barbershop and Salon

1. To develop an understanding of how a barbershop/hair salon operates through practice and simulation

2. To develop oral communication skills through role-playing various roles, such as hair stylist, barber, manicurist, shop owner or manager, cashier, and customer

3. To develop oral communication skills by discussing with the customer what he wants the stylist to do

4. To develop concepts of print by reading product labels, hair and beauty magazines, and the center books (page 73)

5. To reinforce book-handling skills by encouraging children to read the various magazines and books at the center

6. To develop phonemic awareness and letter recognition of the **G** sound in **gel** and the **W** sound in **wig**, and to reinforce the **H** sound in **hair**, the **L** sound in **lotion**, the **C** sound in **comb**, the **R** sound in **razor**, the **N** and **P** sounds in **nail polish**, and the **B** sound in **barber**

7. To develop reading skills by reading environmental print, hair products packaging, and price lists

8. To develop writing skills by creating name tags and writing bills for customers

9. To develop writing skills by dictating a story about a first trip to a barbershop/hair salon

10. To develop math skills by pricing various hair products, counting money, and sequencing the steps to getting a haircut

11. To develop nonstereotypical concepts of gender in the workplace

     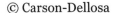

Props

- Hair products (empty shampoo and conditioner bottles, hair spray, styling gel, mousse, hair color boxes)
- Empty nail polish and nail polish remover bottles, emery boards, hand lotion, a small bowl to soak hands, and cotton balls
- Plastic razors, shaving cream containers
- Plastic scissors and plastic tweezers
- Chairs for the waiting room and for the barbershop/hair salon

- Table for reception desk
- Play money, Play debit/credit cards
- Combs, brushes, plastic hair rollers, barrettes, rubber bands, clips, bobby pins, hair picks, hair dryers, cordless hair dryers, curling irons, and mirrors
- Telephone
- Large shirts or smocks
- Large bowls for sinks
- A large tray for nail products

Print Materials

- Center sign with the name of the Barbershop/Hair Salon
- Signs for Open/Closed, Exit, Hours of Operation, No Smoking
- Price list chart with cost of haircut, styling, shave, manicure, pedicure, permanent, and hair coloring
- Name tags for hair stylist, barber, manicurist, owner/manager, and receptionist
- Hair styling magazines

- Calendar and appointment book
- Appointment cards
- Rebus word cards for **G–gel**, **W–wig**, **B–barber**, **and H–hair**
- Chart with pictures of the roles children can play in this center, including hair stylist, barber, manicurist, owner/manager, receptionist, and customer
- Rebus bills and receipts
- "Hair" poem (page 76) written on chart paper

      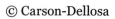

Writing Materials

- Appointment book and appointment cards
- Name tags
- Billing forms and receipts
- Supply order forms
- Pens, pencils, and markers
- Paper to record children's stories

Book List

- *Aaron's Hair* by Robert Munsch (Cartwheel, 2002)
  Aaron is having a bad hair day, so he yells at his hair. This causes his hair to run away, and Aaron has to figure out how to get his hair back.

- *I Love My Hair* by Natasha Anastasia Tarpley (Megan Tingley, 1998)
  A young African-American girl describes how her mom combs the tangles out of her hair.

- *Makeup Mess* by Robert Munsch (Cartwheel, 2002)
  Julie spends all of her money on cosmetics, and her parents are not happy about her purchases.

- *Nappy Hair* by Carolivia Herron (Dragonfly Books, 1998)
  This book focuses on a little girl with nappy hair who discovers why her hair is so curly.

- *Rapunzel* by Paul O. Zelinsky (Dutton Books, 1997)
  In this award-winning Caldecott book, a young girl named Rapunzel lets down her hair so her prince can climb up the tower where she has been imprisoned.

- *Stephanie's Ponytail* by Robert Munsch (Annick Press, 1996)
  Stephanie has her mother fix her ponytail in a variety of ways. All of the children in her class copy Stephanie and fix their hair the same way until…

Storage Container

A large box decorated with pictures of children and adults with various hairstyles, hair products, and nail supplies. Be sure to include an equal number of males and females.

     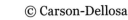

Implementing the Barbershop/Hair Salon

Procedures:

Step 1   Visit a local hair salon and a barbershop to collect free hair-product samples, combs, or other materials that the shop owner is willing to donate. Observe the surroundings carefully to see how the salon and barbershop are set up and note what kinds of literacy materials (signs, charts, posters, etc.) are displayed.

Step 2   Collect or create as many props, print, and writing materials as possible from the props and materials lists. Visit the local library to check out a variety of fiction and nonfiction books.

Step 3   Design a storage box by attaching pictures of children and adults with various hairstyles and ads for hair and nail products to a large box. Download appropriate environmental print and images from the Internet. Create the rebus word cards, price list, name tags, appointment book, appointment cards, billing form, and business cards. Copy the poem "Hair" (page 76) on chart paper using markers to write the color words.

Step 4   Choose an area in the classroom close to the sink so children can use it to pretend to wash their clients' hair. Or make a sink out of a box. (See page 41 for directions.) Create a red, striped pole for the Barbershop by gluing red ribbon or paper to a large dowel rod and attach the name of the Barbershop to the pole. Make a sign for the Hair Salon and hang both of these signs in the center. Put up posters and arrange a series of pictures of people with various haircuts around the center. Post the price list chart. Arrange chairs so that the waiting area is separate from the Barbershop/Hair Salon. Set up a station for the barber to use and one for the hair stylist by placing the appropriate materials/props next to the chairs. Then, arrange the nail products on a tray. Use a table for the cash register, appointment book, telephone, and various hair products that will be sold in this center. Display the magazines in the waiting area.

Step 5   Gather children in the reading area and show them the book *Stephanie's Pony Tail* by Robert Munsch (Annick Press, 1996). Ask them to predict what the story will be about based on the title and the book cover. Read the story aloud, inviting children to join in by repeating the refrain aloud. After reading the story, invite children to discuss hairstyles by asking them to share their experiences. Ask them if they have ever been to a barbershop or hair salon. Then, ask them to tell what the hairstylist/barber does first, second, third, etc. As they describe each step, show them the appropriate hair product (shampoo, conditioner, hair gel, etc.) Record their responses on a chart numbering the steps in order and using rebus pictures. Place this chart in the center.

 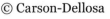

Step 6   Invite children into the Barbershop/Hair Salon by pointing out the red barber pole with the name of the Barbershop and the sign with the name of the Hair Salon. Point out the Hours of Operation sign and ask them if they recognize the word **Open** by pointing to it on the sign and asking for a volunteer to read it and locate it on the word wall. Show them the chart with pictures of the roles children can play in this center, including the hair stylist, the barber, the manicurist, the shop manager, and the receptionist.

Choose five children to help introduce the center and play the roles of shop manager, receptionist, barber, hair stylist, and manicurist. Show them the waiting area with the books and magazines to look at, the chairs to sit in, the posters and pictures of various hairstyles, and the receptionist's area with the appointment book, cash register, telephone, and hair products.

Model what customers do when they enter the shop by telling the receptionist their name and signing the appointment book. Direct the child who was assigned the role of shop manager to greet you and welcome you to her shop. Sit in one of the chairs and read a magazine. Tell the receptionist to call your name and then proceed to introduce yourself to the hairstylist.

The child playing the role of the hairstylist will greet you and introduce him/herself and ask what you would like to have done to your hair. Explain what you want done by referring to a picture of the haircut you chose from the waiting area. Model how to explain exactly what you would like the stylist to do. Encourage the stylist to repeat back what was said. Remind the stylist to refer to the chart with the recorded sequence of getting a haircut. Direct the stylist to follow these steps and pretend to wash your hair, cut it, blow-dry it, and style it with the curling iron. Keep up a running conversation while the stylist is working on your hair. Ask to see a mirror so that you can see the back of your hair. Thank the stylist for your new hairdo. The stylist will then write up the bill by placing a check mark next to **shampoo**, **blow-dry**, and **style** on the billing form.

Proceed next to the manicurist's station, exchange introductions, and decide if you want nail polish. Tell the manicurist to file the nails on your right hand with the emery board, put lotion on your hand, and then place your right hand in the bowl of soapy liquid. Repeat the same steps with your left hand. Then, tell the manicurist to apply nail polish to your fingernails (if you selected this) and use the cotton balls to wipe away any excess polish. (This should be pretend nail polish.) Thank the manicurist for your beautiful nails and ask for the bill. The manicurist will place a check mark next to **manicure** on the bill.

Proceed back to the waiting area and hand the bill to the receptionist. Model how to total up the bill to figure out how much you owe. Show how to count out the money to pay for the bill, or you can hand the receptionist a charge card. Tell the receptionist how to count the money

 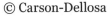

and/or prepare the charge slip and write a receipt. Exchange thank-yous and good-byes with the receptionist and the shop manager. Act out what it would be like to get a shave and a haircut from a barber by adapting the procedures outlined above for a hairstyle and manicure. Tell children how many can play in this center at one time and remind them that the Barbershop/ Hair Salon center will be open for three to four weeks so that everyone will have the chance to play in this center.

Step 7   Write the poem "Hair" on chart paper and share the poem with students. Hand out word cards with the different-color words written on them and one with the word **hair**. Read the title of the poem and compare it to the **hair** card. Point out that both words begin with an **H**. Read the poem aloud and then reread it with children. Invite children who have the word cards to place their cards under the matching color words.

You may want to prepare colorful squares of the four hair colors mentioned in the poem and have children graph their hair color.

> ## Hair
>
> Red hair, black hair,
>
> Yellow hair, brown hair.
>
> What color is your hair?
>
> Curly hair, straight hair,
>
> Long hair, short hair.
>
> What type is your hair?

Step 8   Gather children together in front of the Barbershop/Hair Salon, review the chart, and name the various roles that children can play in this literacy play center. Explain to them that while this center is open, they will have an opportunity to meet with you and tell about their first haircut. These stories will be recorded, transcribed, and placed in a booklet called "Our First Haircuts" so everyone will be able to read them. Children should also be encouraged to draw a self-portrait with a new hairstyle that can be displayed on the walls of the Barbershop/Hair Salon. Review all of the word cards that were introduced in this center.

Step 9   Gather the assessment materials that will be used in this center. In addition to the Socialization Skills Rating Scale (page 137), you will also need the Emergent and Early Writing Rubric (page 141).

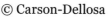

 # Post Office

Goals and Objectives for Children

1. To develop an understanding of how a post office operates through practice and simulation

2. To develop oral communication skills through role-playing various roles, such as mail carrier, package delivery person, postal worker, and customer

3. To develop oral communication skills by selling and purchasing postage stamps, envelopes, and postcards, and shipping packages

4. To develop concepts of print by reading names, addresses, package labels, letters, cards, post cards, junk mail, and the center books (page 79)

5. To reinforce book-handling skills by encouraging children to read the various books at the center

6. To develop phonemic awareness and letter recognition of the **Z** sound in **ZIP code**, the **J** sound in **junk mail**, and to reinforce the **B** sound in **bill**, the **P** sound in **package** and **postage**, the **S** sound in **stamp**, the **L** sound in **letter**, the **M** sound in **mail**, the **E** sound in **enter**, and the **A** sound in **address**

7. To develop reading skills by reading environmental print, addresses, letters, postcards, ZIP code books, and signs

8. To develop writing skills by writing letters, addressing envelopes and postcards, creating name tags and receipts, and designing stamps

9. To practice recognizing and stating their own address

10. To develop math skills by reading and writing numbers in ZIP codes

11. To practice using a scale by weighing packages

12. To practice using dollar bills, quarters, and pennies to buy products

13. To develop cooperative learning skills by interacting with other children at the Post Office

Props

- Tricycle to be used as a mail truck
- Individual mailboxes
- Backpack to carry mail
- Packages and packing materials
- Stamp pad to cancel stamps
- Classroom mailbox
- Scale to weigh letters and packages
- Plastic tray to hold mail
- Play money
- Index cards and a photo album that holds cards of that size
- Cash register
- Peg-board to display stamps and other postal products

Print Materials

- Center sign with the name of the Post Office
- Junk Mail
- Open/Closed Sign
- Magazines
- ZIP Code Book
- Telephone book
- Signs for Open/Closed, Exit, Hours of Operation, No Smoking
- Address cards
- Canceled stamps
- Stickers
- Forms, such as mail forwarding, mail stop
- Stamp charts
- Rebus word cards for **Z–ZIP code**, **J–junk mail**, **B–bill**, **P–package**, **S–stamp**, **M–mail**, **L–letter**, **E–enter**, **and A–address**
- Finger play "The Mail Carrier" (page 82) and the title "Types of Mail" written on chart paper
- Chart with pictures of the roles children can play in this center including mail carrier, package delivery person, postal worker, and customer

Writing Materials

- Pens and pencils
- Greeting cards
- Envelopes
- Postcards
- Stationery
- Checks

Book List

- *A Day with a Mail Carrier* by Jan Kottke (Children's Press, 2000)
  This is a nonfiction book that shows what a mail carrier does at work.

- *Dear Peter Rabbit* by Alma Flor Ada (Aladdin Paperbacks, 1997)
  Famous children's book characters write letters that go beyond their basic stories.

- *Dear Mr. Blueberry* by Simon James (Aladdin, 1996)
  Emily writes to her teacher because she believes there is a whale in her backyard.

- *The Jolly Postman* by Janet and Allan Ahlberg (Little, Brown and Co., 2001)
  An interactive book with a package or letter to a different fairy tale on every page.

- *The Post Office Book: Mail and How It Moves* by Gail Gibbons (HarperTrophy, 1986)
  A step-by-step book about how a letter is delivered.

- *To the Post Office with Mama* by Sue Farrell (Annick Press, 1994)
  A young child walks to the post office on a snowy, cold day.

- *Will Goes to the Post Office* by Olof and Lena Landstrom (R and S Books, 2001)
  Will and the neighborhood children go to the post office to pick up a package from Uncle Ben.

Storage Container

Stamps, envelopes, and other paper products can be stored in a backpack. Larger props can be stored inside the large mailbox. Posters and charts can have two or three holes punched in them and hung from hooks in the classroom or on a chart stand.

Implementing the Post Office

Procedures:

Step 1   Visit a local post office to collect postal envelopes, forms, and print material that can be donated. Look at the different types of products that are displayed (signs, posters, stamps, packages, etc.).

Step 2   Collect or create as many props, print, and writing materials as possible from the props and materials lists. Visit the local library to check out books. Be sure to get some nonfiction books.

Step 3   Download appropriate environmental print and signs from the Internet. Paint a large cardboard box blue and add a postal logo to create a large mailbox. Use red and white letters to spell out **Mail**. Shoe boxes or tissue boxes can be made into individual mailboxes. Cut a slot on the top of the box for the mail to be delivered and an opening on the side of the box for children to retrieve their mail. Write a child's name on each individual mailbox. Create address cards by writing children's names and addresses on small individual index cards. Take pictures of each child and place a small picture of the child on each address card. The cards can be used by children to address their mail. Write the finger play "The Mail Carrier" (page 82) on chart paper. Remember to leave space between each line for children to match the words. Cut sticker paper into rectangles to be used by children to create their own stamps. Create a stamp poster to show children different stamp designs.

Step 4   Choose an area in the classroom close to the Housekeeping center. Use a table to create a counter for the Post Office. Place a basket behind the table for the postal worker to place the mail. A large display board placed behind the counter could be used to display stamps, envelopes, and postcards for purchase. Set up another table with a ZIP code book and pen for customers to address envelopes. Place the large mailbox near the entrance to the post office. The individual mailboxes should be placed in a convenient location away from the post office. Write a postcard to children and mail it in sufficient time for it to arrive to introduce the Post Office.

Step 5   Introduce the center by gathering children and show them the postcard that was delivered by the postal carrier. Read the postcard to children.

Then, inquire how the postal carrier knows where to deliver the mail. Show children the address on the front of the postcard and read it aloud. Tell children that this is the address of their school. Show children the word card for **address** and point out the initial letter **A**. Ask children what other words they remember that start with **A**. Point to the group of numbers at the end of the address and tell children these numbers are called the ZIP code. Explain that the ZIP code is a

 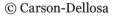

special set of numbers that helps the post office deliver the mail to the correct city or town. Show children the word card for **ZIP code**, and ask them to repeat the words **ZIP code**. Point to each word as it is read. Have children count the words on the card. Point out that ZIP starts with the **Z** sound and have children make the **Z** sound. Point to the word card for **code** and ask what letter it begins with. Have children identify other words that start with **C**. Ask a volunteer to place the words **ZIP code** on the word wall. Point out this is the first word on the wall under the letter **Z**.

Step 6   Play a game to help children learn their home address. Have children sit in a circle. Remind them of the postcard they received and ask if they remember how the letter carrier knew where to deliver the postcard. Explain that everyone has an address that tells where they live. Ask children to raise their hand if they know their address. Tell children that they are going to play a game to help them remember their address. To play the game, children must listen carefully to the address that is said. The child whose address is read must stand up and say, "I live at _____." and repeat the address. If children do not recognize their address, tell the child that it is his/her address and help the child repeat the address. Once the child stands up and repeats the address, the child will be given his/her address card to hold until everyone has had a turn. Use the address cards previously created to play the game. Collect the cards at the end so that the game can be played again at a later time and used in the center.

Step 7   Generate a discussion by asking children what kind of mail they receive at home. As children name different types of mail (letter, bill, card, junk mail, magazine, package), write the words on a chart labeled "Types of Mail." Be sure to have samples of the different types of mail to show children and place them next to the words on the chart. Help children identify the **L** sound in **letter**, the **B** sound in **bill**, the **M** sound in **mail** and **magazine**, and the **P** sound in **package** as you write the words on the chart. Tell children that **junk** starts with the **J** sound. Show children the word card for **junk mail** and point out the **J** sound. Ask if there are any children whose names start with **J**. Ask them to count the number of words in **junk mail**. Ask them what other card on the word wall has two words on it (ZIP code). Then, show children the word card for **bill** and ask someone to find that word on the chart. Repeat this procedure for **mail** and **package**. Place the word cards on the word wall.

Step 8　Place the chart paper finger play "The Mail Carrier" where children can see it. Read the finger play to children, tracking the print as you read.

Show children the word card for **mail** and ask someone to match it to the word **mail** on the chart. Ask someone to find the word on the word wall. Chant all of the words under **M** on the word wall. Read the finger play again and ask if anyone can identify the rhyming words. After **blue** and **you** are identified as rhyming, ask all of the children to say the two words. Ask if anyone knows another word that rhymes with **blue** and **you**.

> The Mail Carrier
>
> See the mail carrier
>
> Dressed in blue
>
> Bringing lots of mail
>
> To me and you.

Step 9　Read *Will Goes to the Post Office* by Olaf and Lena Landstrom (R and S Books, 2001). Read the title and the author. Read the story aloud, stopping to discuss important facts. After the story, show children the postcard again and point to the stamp. Ask if anyone remembers what it is called. Explain that people must put a stamp on items they mail. Use the stamp chart to show children some of the different kinds of stamps. Talk about the pictures on the stamps. Tell children they may also make their own stamps for their post office. Show them the precut rectangles of sticker paper. Point out the shape of the paper and tell them it is a rectangle. Give each child a piece of the sticker paper and let them design a stamp. Collect the stamps to be used in the Post Office. Tell children the paper will be available for them to create additional stamps. Show them where to locate the paper and where to place the completed stamps for the Post Office.

Step 10　Introduce the center by pointing out the sign for the Post Office. Point out the Enter sign above the entrance to the Post Office. Tell them that this sign tells us where to go into a building, store, or office. Show the word card for **Enter** and have children place it on the word wall. Take children on a tour of the Post Office. Show children where to purchase the stamps, envelopes, etc. and model how to buy the merchandise using pennies, quarters, and dollar bills. Encourage them to compare the size and color of the quarters and pennies. Show children the large mailbox and model how to mail the letter.

Show children a package that needs to be mailed. Point out that packages are not placed in the mailbox because they must be weighed to find out how much they cost to mail. Model how the postal worker will weigh the package on the scale. Show children the numbers on the scale. Demonstrate how to read the scale. Tell children that the postal worker will sell the correct number of stamps for the package. The package will need the same number of stamps as the number on the scale.

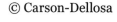

Tell children that the postal workers put a mark on the stamp to show that it has been used. Show them the stamper they will use to put a mark on the postage stamp. Tell them that the postal worker will mark each piece of mail before it can be delivered. Give an addressed letter to a child to mail. Model how the postal worker will collect the mail, cancel the stamp, and place the mail in a tray for the mail carrier to collect. Have a child collect the mail from the tray and place it in the mail pouch. Explain that the mail carrier can either walk to deliver the mail or drive the mail truck (tricycle). Model how the mail carrier must read the name on the envelope to deliver the mail. Ask children to find the individual mailboxes in the classroom and demonstrate how the mail carrier will deliver the mail to each mailbox.

Step 11 Before opening the Post Office, demonstrate how to use the name cards to address mail to classmates. Place the address cards in a photo album that holds that size of cards and set the address book on the table in the Post Office. Share the rest of the props that have been placed in the center. Tell them the center will be open for three to four weeks so that everyone will have a chance to play in it. Remind them of the established procedures for playing in the center. Review all of the word cards for this center. Show children the various books that have been placed in the center and encourage them to read these books while this center is open.

Step 12 Gather the assessment materials that will be used in this center and place them in a convenient location near the Post Office. The assessment instruments needed are Socialization Skills Rating Scale (page 137), Alphabet Knowledge Assessment (page 138) (review B, F, L, P, M, T, S, K, H, E, D, N, C, I, X, Q, O, V, R, A, G, W, Z, J), Number Recognition Assessment (page 140), and Emergent and Early Writing Rubric (page 141).

 # Florist Shop

Goals and Objectives for Children

1. To develop an understanding of how a florist shop operates through practice and simulation

2. To develop oral communication skills through role-playing various roles, such as florist, cashier, store manager, delivery person, and customer

3. To develop oral communication skills by greeting customers and taking and delivering orders

4. To develop concepts of print by reading seed packets, catalogs, and the center books (page 86)

5. To develop book-handling skills by encouraging children to read the various center books and examine the catalogs in the center

6. To develop phonemic awareness and letter recognition of the **Y** sound in **yellow**, and to reinforce the **F** sound in **flowers**, the **P** sound in **plants**, the **D** sound in **delivery**, the **R** sound in **rose**, and the **G** sound in **garden**

7. To develop reading skills by reading environmental print and rebus signs for the types of flowers and flower arrangements

8. To develop writing skills by writing customers' orders, bills, and delivery information

9. To develop math skills by counting the correct number of flowers to deliver, sorting flowers and plants, and counting money

10. To develop color recognition by sorting flowers by color

11. To develop the ability to name the stem, leaf, and flower of a plant by matching word cards to a chart

12. To practice being a gardener by growing seeds

13. To develop cooperative learning skills by interacting with other children at the Florist Shop

     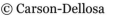

Props

- Yellow, red, pink, white, blue, and purple plastic/silk flowers and plants
- Flower seed packets
- Flowerpots and vases
- Baskets
- Play money and Play debit/credit cards
- Cash register
- Flower arrangement area
- Plastic bins
- Watering can/pitcher, spray bottle, plant mister
- Foam forms or play dough to put flowers and plants in
- Telephone
- Vehicle (or wagon) to deliver flowers
- Seeds, soil
- Plastic cups
- Boxes for delivering flowers

Print Materials

- Center sign with the name of the Florist Shop
- Poster with pictures and names of flowers and plants
- Flower Arrangement chart
- Word cards with flower and plant names
- Chart with picture of parts of a plant labeled and the word cards **roots**, **stem**, **leaf**, **and flower**
- Rebus flower arrangement order forms
- Flower/plant catalog
- Calendar
- Signs for Open/Closed, Exit, Hours of Operation, No Smoking
- Price tags for flower arrangements
- FTD® sign
- Bills, receipts, and charge slips
- Rebus word cards for **Y–yellow**, **F–flowers**, **P–plants**, **D–delivery**, **R–rose**, **G–garden**
- A chart with the pictures of the various roles children can play in the center, including flower arranger, manager, and delivery person
- Song "The Florist in the Shop" and finger play "The Florist Shop" (page 89) written on chart paper

Writing Materials

- Pens and pencils
- Order pads
- Bills, receipts, and charge slips
- Checks
- Note cards
- Name cards
- Erasable markers

Book List

- *The Flower Alphabet Book* by Jerry Pallotta (Charlesbridge, 1988)
  Bright, bold, colorful illustrations of flowers from A to Z are combined with simple text to tell about flowers.

- *Flower Garden* by Eve Bunting (Voyager Books, 2000)
  An urban, African-American girl and her father buy plants, potting soil, and a window box at the supermarket, ride the bus to their apartment, and put together a colorful gift for the child's mother.

- *Fran's Flower* by Lisa Bruce (HarperCollins, 2000)
  Fran finds a flowerpot filled with soil and decides to grow a flower. She decides to try to feed the flower a variety of different things.

- *One Bean* by Anne Rockwell (Walker Books for Young Readers, 1999)
  A young child describes what happens as a bean grows on a wet paper towel. Bold, accurate illustrations accompany the text.

- *Planting a Rainbow* by Lois Ehlert (Voyager Books, 1992)
  Mother and child plant a rainbow as they plant bulbs, order seeds, and select seedlings.

- *Sunflower House* by Eve Bunting (Voyager Books, 1999)
  A young boy plants sunflower seeds in a circle and waits patiently while they grow taller than him, making a perfect sunflower house.

- *This Is the Sunflower* by Lola M. Schaefer (Greenwillow Books, 2000)
  A cumulative rhyme about the life cycle of a sunflower. Gorgeous watercolor illustrations combine realistic images with imagination.

- *The Tiny Seed* by Eric Carle (Aladdin, 2001)
  Children learn how seeds travel and grow into plants.

  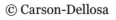

Storage Container

A wagon that doubles as the flower delivery vehicle could be used to store the silk/plastic flowers and plants, the flowerpots and vases, and other large items. Writing materials, play money, and catalogs could be stored in a crate. Posters and charts can have two or three holes punched in them and hung from hooks in the classroom or on a chart stand.

Implementing the Florist Shop

Procedures:

Step 1   Visit local florist shops to collect empty seed packets, plant catalogs, plastic/silk flowers and plants, and pots. Florist shops may be willing to donate additional items if asked. Look at the various types of signs that are displayed (flower arrangements, flower/plant charts). If possible, arrange for children to take a field trip to a florist shop. If that is not possible, try to arrange for a florist to visit children and share information about his/her career and model how to create a flower arrangement.

Step 2   Collect or create as many props, print, and writing materials as possible from the props and materials lists. Parents may have silk/plastic flowers or plants, flowerpots, or seed packets that they would donate. Visit the local library to check out books. Be sure to get some nonfiction books on flowers and plants. Books by the National Audubon Society are especially useful because of the beautiful pictures.

Step 3   Download appropriate environmental print and images from the Internet. Create two charts, one with pictures of different flowers labeled and one with different plants labeled. Create a chart that has a simple illustration of parts of a plant and label the roots, stem, leaves, and flower. Place a piece of Velcro® above the labels on the chart. Make word cards for **roots**, **stem**, **leaves**, and **flower** and place Velcro® on the back. These will be placed over the words on the chart. Write the song and finger play on chart paper. Remember to leave space between the lines when writing the finger play. Laminate the finger play so that children will be able to use a washable marker on it. On the Internet, find pictures of flower arrangements that can be delivered. Print out the

names and pictures of the flower arrangements, place them in a notebook, and put the book in the center. Design the rebus order chart, order pads, signs, and other print materials. Create three or four flower arrangements and attach price tags to these. Arrange flowers in two or three vases, attach price tags, and place them in the shop. Put price tags on these.

Step 4   Choose an area in the classroom to set up the Florist Shop. Select an area that is near a window for sunlight to grow the plants. Hang the Florist Shop sign and display the posters. Arrange the furniture and storage containers for the different flowers and plants. Use a table for the sales counter and place the calendar, flower arrangement notebook, order slips, cash register, and telephone there. Set up an area for children to create flower arrangements. Place the flower arrangements and vases already created on display in the Florist Shop.

Step 5   Prior to introducing the center, gather children in a circle and show them the silk/plastic flowers placed in a large basket. Ask children if they remember what letter makes the beginning sound in **flowers**. If they do not remember, tell them that flowers begins with **F**. Model and have them make the **F** sound aloud. Show them the word card for **flowers**, have children read it and place it on the word wall. Ask children if they can think of other words that start with **F**. Be sure to include the names of children in the class that begin with **F**.

Take out a yellow rose from the large basket and have children identify the color. Ask them what letter **yellow** begins with and invite a child to make the **Y** sound. Have children repeat the **Y** sound and read the word card for **yellow** aloud. Generate a list of other words that begin with **Y**.

Ask children if they know the name of the yellow flower. If necessary tell them it is called a **rose**. Show children the word card **rose** and read it with them. Ask a child to find all of the roses in the basket. Repeat the procedure with other flowers in the basket. Point out the color and beginning sound for each flower. Read *The Flower Alphabet Book* by Jerry Pallotta (Charlesbridge, 1988) to children. As the book is read, point out and discuss the illustrations bordering the flowers. Ask children to name some of the flowers in the book. Tell them they need to remember the names of the flowers to play a game later.

Show children the chart with the song "The Florist in the Shop" (page 89). Read the title and the first verse of the song tracking the print as it is read. Sing the first verse to the tune of "The Farmer in the Dell" with children. Then, read the second verse, tracking the print, and sing it with children.

Tell children they are going to play a game that goes along with the song. Ask children to stand, join hands, and make a circle. Select a child to be the florist who goes into the center of the circle. Explain that everyone will sing the first two verses. At the end of the second verse, the florist will select a child to be the rose. The rose will join the florist in the center of the circle. Sing the song and play the game with children. After the rose goes into the circle, ask a child to name another flower. Sing the second verse again, substituting the new flower for the rose. Continue playing the game until several types of flowers have been named and then sing the final verse of the song.

The (flower) stands alone,
The (flower) stands alone,
Heigh-ho the derry-o
The (flower) stands alone.

The Florist in the Shop
(sung to tune of "The Farmer in the Dell")

The florist in the shop,

The florist in the shop,

Heigh ho the derry-o,

The florist in the shop.

The florist picks a rose,

The florist picks a rose,

Heigh ho the derry-o,

The florist picks a rose.

Step 6   Generate a conversation about floral shops by asking questions like, *Who can share a time they went to buy flowers? What are some things that can be purchased at a florist shop? Has anyone ever had flowers delivered to their home?* If children have had limited experiences with a florist shop, read a book and show children pictures of floral shops printed from the Internet. Discuss the story and pictures.

Step 7   Show children the finger play "Florist Shop" that has been written on chart paper. Read it to them, pointing to each word as it is read. Read it again and ask children to join in. Point to the word **flowers** on the finger play. Ask a volunteer to read the word aloud and find it on the word wall. Have children circle the word **flowers** on the chart with an erasable marker.

Next, show children the word card **yellow** and read it together. Select another child to match the word card to the word **yellow** on the chart. Place the word card on the word wall.

Reread the finger play. Point to and read the words **too** and **you** again. Ask children why these words are underlined. If necessary point out that these are rhyming words because they sound alike.

Florist Shop

Red flowers, yellow flowers,

Purple flowers <u>too</u>

All ready

To be sent to <u>you</u>.

Step 8 Read *One Bean* by Anne Rockwell (Walker Books for Young Readers, 1999) and place a bean seed and a wet paper towel in a resealable plastic bag. Show children the poster with the roots, stem, leaves, and flower labeled. Point to the various parts of the plant, name them, and have children read the words aloud. Show children the word card **roots** and ask for a volunteer to match the word card to the word on the chart. Have the child place the word card over the label by connecting the Velcro® on the word card with the Velcro® on the chart. Repeat for the remaining words. Tell children the chart will be in the Florist Shop for them to use again.

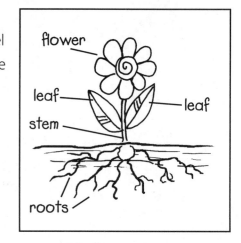

Explain to children they will be able to observe the development of roots, stem, and leaf as the bean plant grows in the resealable plastic bag.

Step 9 Explain to children that all plants need sun, soil, and water to grow. On a sheet of paper titled "What Plants Need to Grow," write the words **sun**, **soil**, and **water**. Show children a picture of the sun and ask a volunteer to place the picture next to the correct word. Repeat this with pictures of soil and water. Help children plant flower seeds in plastic cups. Show children the watering can/pitcher and plant mister. Tell children they will need to water their plants when the soil is dry. Have children place the plants in a sunny spot in the Florist Shop. Hang the "What Plants Need to Grow" poster nearby. Tell children a person who grows plants is called a gardener. Show them the word card **gardener** and ask for a volunteer to identify the beginning sound. Place the word card on the word wall and read the **G** words on the word wall.

Step 10 Introduce the center by showing children the sign for the Florist Shop. Point out the flower arrangements and the flowers in the shop that are for sale. Ask a child to select a flower arrangement to purchase. Model how the cashier reads the price and writes out a receipt. Have the child pretend to pay for the flowers. Demonstrate how the cashier rings up the sale.

Show children the chart that has different flower arrangements that can be ordered. Explain that sometimes people order flowers for others who live far away. Point out the FTD® sign and explain that florists with an FTD® sign can send flowers anywhere in the world. Model how to take a telephone order by recording the customer's request on the order form. Add up the cost of the flowers and tell the customer the amount due. Demonstrate how to write the credit card information to charge the purchase. Create the flower arrangement.

 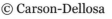

Show children the wagon to use to deliver flowers. Model how to place flower orders in a box for delivery. Show children the word card **delivery**. Ask a child to identify the beginning letter and make its sound. Place the word card on the word wall. Read all of the words that start with **D**.

Step 11 Before opening the Florist Shop center, review the rules that are posted in the classroom. Remind children to sign the role chart and create a name tag. Tell them how many children can play in the center at one time and that the center will be open for three to four weeks so that everyone in the class will have an opportunity to assume the different roles. Review all of the word cards for this center. Show children the various books that have been placed in the center and encourage them to read these books while the Florist Shop is open.

Step 12 Collect the assessment materials that will be used in this center and place them in a convenient location, including Rhyming Words Assessment (page 142) and the Socialization Skills Rating Scale (page 137).

    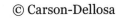

Sporting Goods Store

Goals and Objectives for Children

Preschool Sporting Goods

1. To develop an understanding of how a sporting goods store operates through practice and simulation

2. To develop oral communication skills through role-playing various roles, such as cashier, department manager, salesclerk, stock clerk, and customer

3. To develop oral communication skills by greeting customers, asking for specific products, purchasing materials, and talking to customers or employees

4. To develop concepts of print by reading sales flyers, sports logos, sporting goods products, and the center books (page 94)

5. To develop book-handling skills by reading the various books in the center

6. To develop phonemic awareness and letter recognition of the **U** sound in **umbrella**, and to reinforce the **J** sound in **jump rope**, the **K** sound in **kite**, the **M** sound in **mitt**, the **B** sound in **bat** and **ball**, the **R** sound in **racket**, the **G** sound in **golf**, and the **Y** sound in **yo-yo**

7. To review rhyming words through the use of pictures and word cards

8. To develop the ability to identify parts of a word by clapping out syllables in names and words associated with the Sporting Goods Store

9. To develop reading skills by reading environmental print, rebus signs, and flyers

10. To develop writing skills by creating orders, shopping lists, and bills

11. To develop the ability to classify equipment and clothes by sport

12. To develop the ability to seriate by sorting balls according to size

13. To review the triangle by identifying the shape of a pennant

14. To develop counting and number recognition through 10

15. To reinforce color recognition by identifying and sorting golf balls by color

16. To develop cooperative learning skills by interacting with other children in the Sporting Goods Store

Props

- Basketballs, footballs, softballs, tennis balls, soccer balls, and golf balls of different colors
- Shuttlecocks and tennis/badminton rackets
- Helmets, knee and elbow pads
- Skates
- Kites, yo-yos, and jump ropes
- Golf clubs and umbrellas

- Baskets
- Team pennants
- Hats and shirts with team names
- Bats, baseball mitts
- Wastebasket
- Cash register
- Play money
- Play debit/credit cards

Print Materials

- Center sign with the name of the Sporting Goods Store
- Sports cards
- Pennants
- Team posters
- Paper shirts with team logos
- Labels for various sport departments, such as football, baseball, basketball, soccer, golf, recreation
- Newspaper ads
- Sales signs
- Bags
- Sports magazines, such as *Sports Illustrated* and *SI for Kids*

- Signs for Open/Closed, Exit, Hours of Operation
- Labels for the different products for sale
- Plastic cups with team logos
- Charts for "Golf," "Football," and "Basketball"
- Chart with pictures of the various roles children can play in the center, including cashier, department manager, salesclerk, stock clerk, and customer
- Rebus word cards for **J–jump rope, K–kite, Y–yo-yo, U–umbrella, M–mitt, F–football, G–golf, T–tennis, H–hockey, B–bat, B–ball, R–racket**

 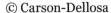

Writing Materials

- Pens and pencils
- Order pads
- Shopping lists
- Name tags

- Bills, receipts, and charge slips
- Inventory list
- Charge slips

Book List

- *Baseball 1, 2, 3* by James Buckley (DK Publishing, 2001)
  Using things associated with baseball, this colorful counting book will engage young readers.

- *Baseball ABC* by Florence Cassen Mayers (Harry N. Abrams, Inc., 1994)
  Using team logos and familiar baseball objects, each letter of the alphabet is illustrated.

- *Baseball A, B, C* by James Buckley (DK Publishing, 2001)
  A colorful alphabet book based on baseball will appeal to young readers.

- *The Baseball Counting Book* by Barbara Barbieri McGrath (Charlesbridge, 1999)
  Baseball terminology is used to help children count from 1 to 20 in this rhyming book.

- *The Baseball Star* by Fred G. Arrigg, Jr. (Troll Communications, 1995)
  The whole town turns out to watch the championship game.

- *Basketball A, B, C: The NBA Alphabet* by Florence Cassen Mayers (Harry N. Abrams, Inc., 1996)
  Color photographs of basketball scenes illustrate each letter of the alphabet.

- *Curious George Plays Baseball* by Margret Rey (Houghton Mifflin, 1986)
  The perennial favorite monkey gets into mischief playing baseball, but becomes the hero of the game.

- *Froggy Plays Soccer* by Jonathan London (Puffin, 2001)
  Froggy joins the Dream Team and plays for the City Cup. Sound effects and repetitive refrain make this book appealing.

- *Kite Flying* by Grace Lin (Dragonfly Books, 2004)
  A Chinese family shops for materials and makes a dragon kite, which they fly on a windy day.

- *My Basketball Book* by Gail Gibbons (HarperCollins, 2000)
  This book introduces basketball equipment, the court, positions of players, and a few rules with easy-to-understand text and brightly colored artwork.

 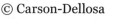

- *My Football Book* by Gail Gibbons (HarperCollins, 2000)
  This book introduces football equipment, the field, positions of players, and a few rules with easy-to-understand text and brightly colored artwork.

- *My Soccer Book* by Gail Gibbons (HarperCollins, 2000)
  This book introduces soccer equipment, the field, positions of players, and a few rules with easy-to-understand text and brightly colored artwork.

- *NFL: Big and Small* (DK Publishing, Inc., 1999)
  A lift-the-flap book introducing size.

- *NFL: Colors* (DK Publishing, Inc., 2000)
  A lift-the-flap book introducing colors.

- *This Is Baseball* by Margaret Blackstone (Henry Holt and Company, 1997)
  Bright pictures and simple text introduce young children to a baseball game.

- *Z is for Zamboni: A Hockey Alphabet* by Matt Napier (Sleeping Bear Press, 2002)
  A rhyming alphabet book using hockey as its theme. The author uses Canadian spelling as a tribute to the origins of the game.

Storage Container

Use a sports-shaped toy box or large boxes decorated with illustrations of sports equipment. Posters and charts can have two or three holes punched in them and be hung from hooks in the classroom or on a chart stand.

     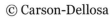

Implementing the Sporting Goods Store

Procedures:

Step 1   Visit local sporting good stores to see how they are arranged. Collect posters, flyers, and other printed materials the stores may be willing to donate.

Step 2   Collect or create as many props, print, and writing materials as possible from the props and materials lists. Newspapers usually have advertisement booklets in the Sunday paper that can be used in the Sport Goods Store. Visit the local library to check out books related to sports. Remember to get some nonfiction books.

Step 3   Download appropriate environmental print to use in the center. Be sure to print several copies of team logos. Team logos can be used to create pennants, signs, cups, and paper clothing. Create pictures of different items associated with sports, including golf clubs and golf balls, football helmet and football pads, baseball bat and mitt, tennis racket and headband to be used in a matching game. Be sure to include two items for each sport. Write the finger plays (page 97) on chart paper leaving space between the lines. Create signs for the store departments by writing the words on poster board and attaching a picture.

Step 4   Select an area in the room to set up the Sporting Goods Store and place the department signs in the store. Arrange shelves or tables and place some of the equipment in the sections, but leave other items for children to place. Use a table for the check-out counter. Place the cash register and bags there.

Step 5   Gather children together close to the Sporting Goods Store center. Show children the sports toy box or decorated boxes and ask them to predict what is inside. Pull out a ball and ask children what letter **ball** begins with and ask them to recall other words that start with **B**. Have children identify what type of ball it is. Write the name of the ball and draw a picture of it on chart paper that is titled "Kinds of Balls." Continue this process until children have identified all of the types of balls.

Generate a conversation about the different games played with the balls. Ask questions about how to play the game, what equipment is used, and experiences children have had playing the games.

Step 6   Place the pictures created for the matching game into a football helmet. Ask children to pull out a picture from the helmet. Have children identify the picture and read the word below it. Ask children to identify the sport associated with the item. For example, a bat goes with a baseball.

Attach the picture below the correct ball on the chart titled "Kinds of Balls." Reinforce the beginning sounds for each word. Show children word cards for **bat**, **ball**, **mitt**, and **racket**, read the words, and have children place the words on the word wall.

Step 7   Show children the finger play "Golf" written on chart paper and ask a volunteer to match the word card **golf** to the word on the finger play. Place the card on the word wall. Read the finger play once, tracking the print as it is read. Select a child to track the print. Ask children to read it aloud while the child tracks the print. Help children identify the two rhyming words in the finger play.

> Golf
> Putt the ball
> Watch it roll
> If you're good
> It's in the hole.

Show children a basket with different-colored golf balls in it. Ask children to sort the golf balls by color. Next, show them different-colored golf tees. Have children match golf tees and golf tees by color.

Use the following finger plays to practice identifying rhyming words during the time the Sporting Goods Store is open.

> Football
> Pass the ball
> And run, run, run,
> Playing football
> Is so much fun.

> Basketball
> Dribble, dribble,
> Shoot the ball,
> Through the net
> Watch it fall.

Step 8   Point out the large signs that identify the different sections of the Sporting Goods Store already placed in the center. Invite children to name the items already placed in the sections. From the sports toy box or decorated box, ask children to select an item and place it in the correct section. For the recreation center, include a jump rope, a yo-yo, and a kite. When children select the jump rope, show them the word card and ask them to count the number of words on the

     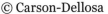

card. Ask them to locate another word card on the wall that begins with **J** and has two words. Read the word from the word wall. Place the word card **jump rope** on the word wall. When children select the kite, show them the word card, have them read it, and place the word card on the word wall. Repeat the same procedure for **yo-yo**.

Continue to have children select and place items on the shelves in the correct department. When the umbrella is selected, explain that golfers carry an umbrella with them in case it rains. Tell children that **umbrella** starts with the **U** sound. Make the sound and ask children to repeat it. Show children the word card for **umbrella**. Have children read the word aloud and place it on the word wall. Identify children that have a **U** in their name and have children say the names.

Step 9   Ask children if they know the names of any sports teams. Write the name of the team on a pennant cut out of card stock. Read the name with children. Select the correct team logo downloaded previously and attach it to the pennant. Help children identify additional names of sports teams and create pennants for these teams. The pennants can be placed in the Sporting Goods Store for sale. Ask children if they know what shape the pennant is. When they identify a triangle, count the number of sides on the pennant. Ask children what else has the shape of a triangle.

Step 10 Tell the students that their Sporting Goods Store has a game that customers can play. Show children the waste basket in which there is a variety of different-size balls. Tell children that the customers are to take the balls out of the basket and line them up from smallest to largest.

Step 11 Identify the different roles children can play in the center. Model how a salesclerk directs a customer to the correct section of the Sporting Goods Store. Have one child demonstrate how the cashier rings up the sale and demonstrate how the customer pays cash or uses a charge card. Use dollars and pennies to help children count to 10.

Step 12 Hang a pocket chart at children's eye level. Prepare a sentence strip that says Parts of a Word. On individual index cards write the numbers 1, 2, and 3. Prepare several word cards with the words and a rebus for **football**, **golf**, **tennis**, **hockey**, **umbrella**, **bat**, and **ball**. Bring children's name cards to the circle. Ask children to gather in a circle near the pocket chart. Show children the title on the sentence strip and read it to them. Place this in the top pocket of the pocket chart. Next, show children the number card with 1 written on it and ask children to identify the number. Place the number card on the left side of the second pocket on the pocket chart. Next, show children the number card with 2 written on it. Ask children to identify the number and place the card in the middle of the second pocket. Repeat the procedure for the number 3 and place the card on the right side of the second pocket. Tell children that they are going to be listening

 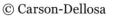

for parts of a word. Show children a name card, read it with children, and clap out the syllables with children. Ask the child to place his/her name card under the correct number on the pocket chart. Repeat this procedure with all of the name cards. After all of the names have been placed on the chart, read each of the one-syllable names again while clapping out the syllable. Repeat the procedure with two and three syllable names.

Show children the word card for **football**, read the card, and have children repeat **football** while clapping out the syllables. Ask a child to place the word card under the correct number. Repeat the activity with additional words, such as **golf**, **tennis**, **hockey**, **umbrella**, **bat**, and **ball**.

Step 13 Before opening the Sporting Goods Store center, review the rules that are posted in the classroom. Remind children to sign the role chart and create a name tag. Tell them how many children can play in the center at one time and that the center will be open for three to four weeks so that everyone will have an opportunity to assume the different roles. Review all of the word cards for this center. Show children the various books that have been placed in the center and encourage them to read these books while this center is open.

Step 14 Gather all of the assessment materials and place them in a convenient location near the Housekeeping Center. All of the assessment instruments may be used in this center. The only new letter to assess on Alphabet Knowledge Assessment (page 138) is **U**.

Home Improvement Store

Goals and Objectives for Children

1. To develop an understanding of how a home improvement store operates through practice and simulation

2. To develop oral communication skills through role-playing various roles, such as cashier, department manager, salesclerk, stock clerk, and customer

3. To develop oral communication skills by greeting customers, helping customers locate materials, and purchasing materials

4. To develop concepts of print by reading advertisements, environmental print, labels, signs, and the center books (page 102)

5. To develop book-handling skills by reading the various books in the center

6. To reinforce phonemic awareness and letter recognition of the **H** sound in **hammer**, the **I** sound in **improvement**, the **T** sound in **tools**, the **L** sound in **lumber**, and the **B** sound in **belt**

7. To develop writing skills by writing orders, bills, and receipts

8. To develop classification skills by stocking shelves with tools and home improvement materials

9. To develop the ability to identify size by matching bolts and washers

10. To develop the ability to recognize a square

11. To develop color recognition by identifying colors of paint

12. To develop the ability to seriate shades of color from lightest to darkest

13. To reinforce the concept of dollar, nickel, and penny by paying for purchases

14. To develop cooperative learning skills by interacting with other children at the Home Improvement Store

 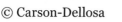

Props

- Plastic hard hats and safety glasses
- Small, medium and large bolts, washers, and nuts
- Scrap lumber (sanded to avoid splinters)
- Wooden building blocks
- Five-pound, plastic ice cream tubs for paint cans
- Foam paintbrushes, paintbrushes, rollers, pans, and paint stirrers
- Drop cloth
- Paint sample cards
- Wallpaper samples and carpet squares
- Various size baskets

- Tools—hammer, screwdriver, pliers, saw, trowels, drills (real or plastic)
- Plastic lawn mower, wheelbarrow, wagon
- Wrapping paper, paper towel, and toilet tissue rolls for pipes
- Cash register
- Play money
- Play debit/credit cards
- Shopping cart
- Paper bags
- Small plastic containers with lids to store bolts, washers, and nuts
- Telephones

Print Materials

- Center sign with the name of the Home Improvement Store
- Department signs, such as Lumber, Wallpaper, Tools, Hardware, Electrical, Appliance, Lawn and Garden
- Sale signs
- Signs for Open/Closed, Exit, Hours of Operation
- Newspaper advertisements and home improvement magazines

- Labels for store items
- Chart with pictures of the roles children can play in this center, including cashier, department manager, salesclerks, stock clerk
- Chart for "Tool Time" (page 104)
- Rebus word cards for **H–hammer, H–hammers, I–improve, T–tools, T–tool belt, L–lumber**

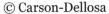

Writing Materials

- Pens and pencils

- Checks

- Bills, receipts, and charge slips

- Name tags

- Blank labels

Book List

- *Architecture Counts* by Michael J. Crosbie and Steve Rosenthal (John Wiley and Sons, 1993)
  Counting from 1–10 using photographs of architecture.

- *Architecture Shapes* by Michael J. Crosbie and Steve Rosenthal (John Wiley and Sons, 1993)
  Photographs of architecture are used to explore shapes through the composition and
  arrangement of windows.

- *B Is for Bulldozer: A Construction ABC* by June Sobel (Gulliver Books, 2003)
  Two children stand outside a fence watching a construction crew work.

- *Bob's Busy Year* by Tricia Boczkowski (Simon Spotlight, 2003)
  Bob the Builder does different work in each season.

- *Builder for a Day* (DK Children, 2003)
  A pop-up book that takes the reader through building a house.

- *Daddy and Me* by Karen Katz (Little Simon, 2003)
  Daddy makes a special project. Looking under the oversized flaps, readers find the tools he
  needs.

- *Old MacDonald Had a Woodshop* by Lisa Shulman (Putnam Juvenile, 2002)
  Old MacDonald is busy building something in her woodshop. Friends and neighbors stop by and
  use various tools to help with the project.

Storage Container

A large box or plastic bin covered with pictures of tools could be used to store the props. Posters and charts can have two or three holes punched in them and be hung from hooks in the classroom or on a chart stand.

Implementing the Home Improvement Store

Procedures:

Step 1   Visit local home improvement stores to collect scrap lumber, sales flyers, and other props the stores are willing to donate. Collect two duplicate card samples of different shades of paint. Look at the various types of signs that are displayed and the different departments within the store.

Step 2   Collect or create as many props, print, and writing materials as possible from the props and materials lists. Visit the local library to check out books. Be sure to get some nonfiction books on construction projects, home improvement, and tools.

Step 3   Download appropriate environmental print and images from the Internet. Create signs for the various departments in the Home Improvement Store. Make the labels for the products that will be on the shelves in the departments. Write the song "Tool Time" (page 104) on chart paper leaving space between the lines. Write the title "Ways to Improve Our Homes" on another piece of chart paper. Make a paper hammer out of construction paper to use for tracking print. If a stove, sink, and refrigerator are not available from the Housekeeping center, paint large cardboard boxes to be a stove, sink, and refrigerator. A washer and dryer can also be made from large cardboard boxes for the appliance section of the store. Line the plastic ice cream buckets with different colors of construction paper to represent paint cans. Cut some of the paint sample cards into individual pieces based on the gradation of color. Place the pieces from a single sample in a resealable plastic bag.

Step 4   Choose an area in the classroom near the Housekeeping center area for the Home Improve-ment Store. Set up a table to be the check-out counter and place the cash register, telephone, bags, and receipts on the table. Hang up signs for the different departments. Place shelves in the departments as necessary and put labels previously created on the shelves to indicate where items belong. Put the appliances, lumber, and lawn and garden supplies in the correct depart-ments.

Step 5   Show children a tool belt that has a hammer, screwdrivers, pliers, and drill on it. Tell them that this is a special belt called a **tool belt** that people sometimes wear when they need to fix things. Show them the word card for **tool belt** and have them count the number of words on the card. Have children find and read other word cards on the word wall that have two words on them. Ask children to identify the beginning letter of **tool** and make the sound. Ask them to do a cheer of the words on the word wall that start with **T**. Ask what letter **belt** begins with and have children make its sound. Read the words that begin with **B** on the word wall.

Take a tool from the belt and ask children to identify it. Assist them if necessary. After each tool is identified, ask children what it is used for and demonstrate proper use of the tool. When the screwdrivers are taken from the belt, show children the difference between a slot and a Phillips screwdriver. Show children different screws and have children select the correct screw for each type of screwdriver.

Show children a book about tools from those collected for the center. Discuss the tools pictured in the book.

Step 6   Show children the finger play "Tool Time" that has been written on chart paper.

Read the title with children and have them name the beginning letters. Read the first verse of the finger play and track the print with a paper hammer as you read. Ask children to read the first verse aloud while doing the actions. Give a child the paper hammer to track the print as you read the second verse.

> **Tool Time**
>
> Peter works with 1 hammer, 1 hammer, 1 hammer
>
> (one fist moving up and down)
>
> Peter works with 1 hammer, now he works with 2.
>
> Peter works with 2 hammers, etc. (two fists)
>
> Peter works with 3 hammers, etc. (two fists and one foot)
>
> Peter works with 4 hammers, etc. (two fists and two feet)
>
> Peter works with 5 hammers, 5 hammers, 5 hammers
>
> (two fists and two feet with head nodding)
>
> Peter works with 5 hammers,
>
> Now his work is done.

Again, have children read the verse aloud the next time. Repeat until all five verses have been read.

Show children the word card for **hammer**. Ask them what letter **hammer** begins with and have them make the sound for **H**. Identify other words that start with **H** and ask them to cheer the **H** words on the word wall. Have children match the word card for **hammer** with the word **hammer** on the chart.

Next, place the word card for **hammers** next to **hammer**. Ask children what is different about the words. Underline the **S** in **hammers**. Have children find the word **hammers** on the chart.

Ask children to point to the number 1 on the chart. Repeat the procedure having them identify the numerals 2–5.

Step 7   Show children the chart with the title "Ways to Improve Our Homes." Read the title with children. Point to the word **improve** and ask children to identify the beginning letter and have them make the sound for "**I**." Read the word aloud and explain that **improve** means to make something better. Show them the word card **improve** and have a child place it on the word wall. Ask children what their parents have done to make their homes look better (paint, mow the lawn) or to fix things that are broken (repair a leaky faucet, replace a window screen). Record children's suggestions on the "Ways to Improve Our Homes" chart.

Ask children where their parents go to buy the items they need to improve their homes or to fix things. Explain that this kind of store is called a Home Improvement Store. Name some of the local home improvement stores in the area.

Step 8   Show children the plastic paint cans with the colorful construction-paper circles and have them identify each color. Take out an intact paint sample card and point out that the sample goes from the lightest to the darkest shade of the color. Then, take its matching paint sample card that has been cut into individual pieces. Lay out the pieces on the floor and ask a child to find the lightest color. Continue until all of the shades of a color have been selected from lightest to darkest. Repeat the procedure with another color. Tell children the paint samples will be in the Home Improvement Store and that they will be able to sort the colors from lightest to darkest when shopping in the store.

Step 9   Gather children in front of the Home Improvement Store. Point to the name of the store and help children read it aloud. Invite children to come into the store. Point out the various departments (Appliances, Paint, Electrical, Hardware, Lumber). As each department is named, identify products that can be found in that section and what they are used for. Ask children to select the correct props and place the items on the shelves that have previously been labeled.

Step 10 Show children a home improvement magazine and explain what can be found inside it. Show them the pictures of houses that have been remodeled and the plans/blueprints for constructing home additions. Talk about what kinds of materials would be needed to make the changes. Two of the most common products needed to remodel a house are lumber and pipes. Point out the sign for the Lumber Department and show children the word card **lumber**. Ask what letter **lumber** begins with and have children make the **L** sound. Model how to purchase lumber. Ask children where they have seen pipes in their homes. Tell children that pipes sometimes need to be replaced and that in a Home Improvement Store the pipes would be located in the Plumbing Department.

     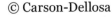

Model how the Paint Department manager helps the customer select a paint color, provides a paint stirrer, and offers to sell paintbrushes, paint rollers, trays, and drop cloths. Select a child to be a customer and have that child take the purchases to the check-out counter. Model how the cashier rings up the bill and how the customer pays with cash or credit. Select another child to play the role of a customer. In the Hardware Department, model how to select bolts, washers, and nuts that match in size and place them in small paper bags for the customer. Point out that the top of the bolt is a square. Compare the square to a rectangle and help children note the sides are all of the same length in a square. Have volunteers select pieces of lumber that are square.

Step 11 Before opening the Home Improvement Store, review the rules that are posted in the classroom. Remind children to sign the role chart and create a name tag. Ask them to count how many children can play in the center at one time. Tell them that the center will be open for three to four weeks so that everyone will have an opportunity to assume the different roles. Review all of the word cards for this center. Show children the various books that have been placed in the center and encourage them to read these books while this center is open.

Step 12 Collect the assessment materials that will be used in this center and place them in a convenient location. These instruments include the Socialization Skills Rating Scale (page 137) and Alphabet Knowledge Assessment (page 138).

 Bank

Goals and Objectives for Children

1. To develop an understanding of how a bank operates through practice and simulation

2. To develop oral communication skills through role-playing various roles, such as bank teller, bank manager, drive-through teller, safe-deposit clerk, security guard, and customer

3. To develop oral communication skills by talking with bank customers and employees

4. To develop concepts of print by reading loan applications, bank withdrawals, deposit forms, and the center books (page 109)

5. To develop book-handling skills by reading the various books and other reading materials in the center

6. To reinforce phonemic awareness and letter recognition of the **B** sound in **bank**, the **T** sound in **teller**, the **M** sound in **money**, the **C** sound in **cash**, the **D** sound in **dollar** and **dime**, the **P** sound in **penny**, the **N** sound in **nickel**, the **A** sound in **ATM**, and the **Z** sound in **zero**

7. To develop recognition of the letters in their own names and in the names of classmates through signatures on documents and bank forms

8. To develop reading skills by reading environmental print and bank forms

9. To develop writing skills by practicing writing withdrawal and deposit slips, ATM slips, and safe-deposit logs

10. To develop math skills by counting money and using an adding machine

11. To develop cooperative learning skills by interacting with other children in the Bank

Props

- Adding machine
- Two cash registers
- Play money and coins
- Telephones
- Display easel for bank literature
- Piggy bank
- Chairs
- Safe-deposit boxes
- Safe-deposit clerk's desk
- Safe
- ATM machine
- Drive-through teller's desk
- Tape to mark the waiting line
- Calendar
- Rubber stamps and a stamp pad
- Tricycles or wagons to use for the drive-through
- A hat and badge for the security guard
- Manager's desk
- Walkie-talkies for the drive-through teller and customers
- Canister (empty potato chip can or other type of can) for drive-through window

Print Materials

- Center sign with the name of the Bank
- Signs for Open/Closed, Exit, Hours of Operation, No Smoking, Line Forms Here
- Deposit envelopes
- ATM slips
- Logbooks
- Checks and debit cards
- Rebus word cards for **B–bank**, **T–teller**, **A–ATM**, **M–money**, **C–cash**, **C–cent**, **D–dollar**, **D–dime**, **P–penny**, **Z–zero**
- Chart with pictures of the roles children can play in this center, including bank teller, bank manager, drive-through teller, safe-deposit clerk, and security guard
- "Money" poem (page 111) written on chart paper

Writing Materials

- Pens, pencils, and markers
- Name tags
- Rebus deposit and withdrawal forms
- Receipt book
- Blank checks
- Labels for safe-deposit boxes
- Savings account book

 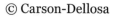

Book List

- *26 Letters and 99 Cents* by Tana Hoban (HarperTrophy, 1995)
  This is two books in one. The first half is about the 26 letters of the alphabet, and the other half focuses on coins and counting money up to 99 cents.

- *Alexander Who Used to Be Rich Last Sunday* by Judith Viorst (Aladdin, 1987)
  Alexander is rich! His grandparents gave him a dollar. He can buy so many things with a dollar—or can he?

- *Bank Tellers: Community Workers* by Cynthia Klingel and Robert B. Noyed (Compass Point Books, 2002)
  This book answers the question, "What does a bank teller do?" Includes duties, skills, physical requirements, and contributions to the community.

- *The Coin Counting Book* by Rozanne Lanczak Williams (Charlesbridge, 2001)
  Children can count coins in rhyme.

- *Follow the Money* by Loreen Leedy (Holiday House, 2003)
  Follow a quarter around for the day from the mint to the bank, around the town, and back to the bank.

- *Just a Piggy Bank* by Gina and Mercer Mayer (Golden Books, 2001)
  Little Critter learns about the importance of saving money.

- *Smart About Money: A Rich History* by Jon Anderson (Grosset and Dunlap, 2003)
  Contains photos of coins and money from all over the world.

Storage Container

A large box decorated to look like an ATM machine could be used to store all of the needed props and materials.

Implementing the Bank

Procedures:

Step 1   Visit a local bank to collect pamphlets and other literature. Look at the various types of literacy materials (signs, charts, etc.) that are displayed. Ask the bank personnel if they have any materials that they are willing to donate.

Step 2   Collect or create as many props, print, and writing materials as possible from the props and materials lists. Visit the local library to check out a variety of fiction and nonfiction books.

Step 3   Download appropriate environmental print, logos, and signs from the Internet. Design the deposit slips and withdrawal forms. Create some savings account books by adding the bank logo to the top of a small notebook or make books with a cover made out of construction paper and blank pieces of paper inside. Use a large cardboard box that has been painted to create the ATM machine. The open end of the box will face the inside of the Bank. On the opposite side, write ATM at the top. Cut four slots, one for deposit, one for withdrawal, a third for the receipts, and the fourth one for the debit card. Label each slot. Cut a flap on the bottom of the box large enough to accommodate envelopes that can be accessed for deposits. Attach a calculator or paint the numbers for the keypad on the box. Create signs to label the departments for the Teller, Loans, Safe-deposit Boxes, and Bank Manager. Copy the "Money" poem (page 111) on chart paper.

Step 4   Choose an area in the classroom and set up the safe-deposit box desk, the drive-through teller area, and the bank manager's desk. Place a large table in the middle of the area and arrange the deposit and withdrawal forms, deposit envelopes, and ATM slips. Use a smaller table for the cashier. Place cash registers at the cashier's table and in the drive-through teller area. Put two chairs in front of the safe-deposit box desk, and the bank manager's desk. Label each desk with the signs. Use tape on the floor to mark the area for the waiting line and post the Line Starts Here sign. Arrange a collection of boxes or plastic storage containers next to the safe-deposit desk. Place the logbook, labels, pens and pencils, and safe-deposit box application forms on the safe-deposit desk. Place an easel with assorted literature next to the bank manager's desk. Place the telephone and a sign that says Bank Manager on this desk. Place the ATM machine next to the drive-through teller's desk. Place the envelopes for the drive-through on the teller's desk.

Step 5   Generate a conversation about banks by asking children where their parents get their money. Then, ask how many of them have ever been to a bank and encourage them to describe what happened at the bank. Be sure to point out that people can get money from a bank and they can also save money in a bank. Show them a sample deposit slip and savings account book. Model how to fill out a deposit slip and make an entry in a savings account book. Then, show them how to fill out a withdrawal form.

Step 6 Choose a book about money from the list and read it to children. Show children the word cards for **money**, **cash**, **nickel**, **dollar**, **dime**, and **penny**. Read the poem "Money" to children.

Allow children to match the word cards for **penny**, **nickel**, and **dime** to the words in the poem. Encourage them to find the words in the poem that rhyme. Empty out a piggy bank that has pennies, nickels, and dimes in it and have children sort the coins. Ask a volunteer to place the matching word card next to the pile of pennies, nickels, and dimes. Show them the other books that will be read to them while the Bank is open.

Step 7 Gather children in front of the Bank center and show them the sign that says Bank. Encourage children to say the word and show them the word card for **bank**. Point out the beginning sound/letter and ask where this word will go on the word wall. Then, show them the chart with the roles that children can play at this literacy play center. Invite them into the bank by turning the Open/Closed sign to Open. Point out the various areas in the bank and

> Money
>
> Penny, penny,
> Easily spent.
> Copper brown
> And worth one cent.
>
> Nickel, nickel,
> Thick and fat,
> You're worth five cents.
> I know that.
>
> Dime, dime,
> Little and thin,
> I remember
> You're worth ten.

show them the labels on each desk. Show them two to three checks that have been created and model how to use the adding machine to figure out the total. Demonstrate how to fill out a deposit slip for the checks as well as a withdrawal slip for $4.00. Point out the numeral **zero**. Show them the word card for zero and ask them to practice making zeroes in the air with their finger. Ask a volunteer to place this word card on the word wall.

Lead children to the cashier's desk and ask a volunteer to play that role. Hand the cashier the deposit slip and tell him/her to stamp it paid. Show children the withdrawal slip and explain that it is used to take money out of the bank. Give the cashier the withdrawal slip for $4.00. Ask him/her to read the number that tells how much money you want to take out of the bank and count out that amount from the cash register. Thank the cashier. Point out the Line Forms Here

     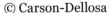

sign and tell children that sometimes people have to wait for someone to help them. This sign tells people where to wait in line.

Take children to the safe-deposit area. Ask for a volunteer to be the safe-deposit clerk and then model how to sign your name into the logbook. Tell the clerk that you want to obtain a safe-deposit box and demonstrate how to fill out the form. Direct the clerk to read back the form to you, give you a safe-deposit box, and make a label for the box with your name. Place the cash in the box and hand it back to the clerk. Show the clerk how to fill out a receipt for the cash. Before leaving the bank, show children the badge and the hat for the security guard and ask them why a bank would need a security guard. Add to their explanation and show them the safe.

Step 8   Explain to children that sometimes people are in a hurry and use the drive-through window. Ask children if they know what happens at a drive-through window. Walk children over to the drive-through area and ask for a volunteer to be the customer. Show them the tricycle or wagon that will be used as a vehicle for the drive-through. Hand the customer a debit card and explain that a customer can either deposit or take out money with this card. Demonstrate how to use the debit or bank card in the ATM to take out money. Next, have another volunteer play the role of the drive-through teller and sit at that desk. Choose another volunteer to be the drive-through customer. Help that child fill out a withdrawal form and proceed to the drive-through and place the withdrawal slip in the canister. Tell the teller to take the canister, read the withdrawal form, and greet the customer by name on the walkie-talkie. The teller should count out the money, place it in the canister, write out a receipt, and return the canister to the customer. The customer should then count the money, thank the teller on the walkie-talkie, and drive away. Tell them that the bank is now closed until tomorrow and turn the Open sign to Closed.

Step 9   Before opening up the Bank for children to play in, review the rules that have been posted in the classroom. Invite children to read the roles chart so they can figure out how many children can play in this center at one time. Remind them that the bank will be open for three to four weeks so that everyone will have a chance to play in it. Review all of the words introduced in this center.

Step 10   Gather the assessment materials that will be used in this center. In addition to the Alphabet Knowledge Assessment (page 138), to check their recognition of all 26 letters, you may also want to use the Number Recognition Assessment (page 140) as well as other assessment materials that apply.

Bakery

Goals and Objectives for Children

Sweet Spot Bakery

1. To develop an understanding of how a bakery operates through practice and simulation

2. To develop oral communication skills through role-playing various roles, such as baker, cake decorator, shop manager, cashier, and customer

3. To develop oral communication skills by talking with the customers and taking phone orders

4. To develop concepts of print by reading recipes, cookbooks, and center books (page 115)

5. To reinforce book-handling skills by reading the various books in the center

6. To reinforce phonemic awareness and letter recognition of the **D** sound in **doughnut** and **dozen**, the **B** sound in **baker**, the **C** sound in **cake**, **coffee**, and **cocoa**, and the **G** sound in **glazed**

7. To develop reading skills by reading environmental print, recipes, and menus

8. To develop writing skills by filling out customers' orders, creating name tags and store signs, designing menus, and writing bills for customers

9. To develop the concept of dozen and half dozen by counting the correct number of baked goods

10. To develop math skills by working with money and pricing baked goods

11. To develop math skills by measuring, reading numbers on measuring cups and spoons, and setting the timer

12. To develop cooperative learning skills by interacting with other children in the Bakery

    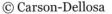

Props

- Measuring cups and spoons
- Serving trays
- Paper plates and straws
- Plastic and paper drink cups
- Cash register
- Play money
- Cookie trays, cupcake, cake, muffin, and bread pans
- Deep fryer
- Tongs and spoons
- Mixing bowls
- Empty flour and sugar containers
- Empty yeast packages
- Rolling pin
- Circle-shaped cutter
- Timer

- Doughnut and cake boxes
- Hats for the bakers
- Paper napkins
- Coffee pot
- Hot cocoa pot
- Plastic bag for the icing
- Paper confetti for sprinkles
- Empty cream and sugar packages
- Play dough for doughnuts and cookies
- Cupcake papers
- Empty cake, bread, muffin, and dessert boxes
- Plastic trays to display the baked goods
- Pictures of different types of bread from the book *Bread, Bread, Bread* by Ann Morris (HarperTrophy, 1993)

Print Materials

- Center sign with the name of the Bakery
- Signs for Open/Closed, Exit, Hours of Operation, No Smoking
- Menus with products and prices
- A large sign with pictures of various baked goods (doughnuts, cakes, cupcakes, bread, and muffins) and their prices
- Bills/receipts
- Rebus recipes for cake, bread, muffins, doughnuts
- Name tags

- Rebus word cards for **C–cake**, **C–cookies**, **D–doughnut**, **D–dozen**, **G–glazed**, **C–coffee**, **C–cocoa**
- A chart with pictures of the various roles children can play in this center, including baker, cake decorator, shop manager, cashier, and customer
- "Little Doughnuts" (page 117) written on chart paper
- "The Muffin Man" (page 117) written on chart paper

   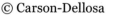

Writing Materials

- Pens, pencils, and markers
- Order pads
- Name tags

- Daily special board
- Labels for pricing the baked goods
- Receipts

Book List

- *Bread, Bread, Bread* by Ann Morris (HarperTrophy, 1993)
  What kind of bread do you eat? All around the world, everyone eats bread. Children can learn about several different types of bread.

- *Bunny Cakes* by Rosemary Wells (Puffin, 2000)
  Ruby is making a cake, and she sends Max to the store with a note listing the ingredients.

- *The Donut Book* by Sally Levitt Steinberg (Storey Publishing, 2004)
  This would make a great reference book for children.

- *Ella Takes the Cake* by Carmela D'Amico (Arthur A. Levine Books, 2005)
  Ella the elephant wants to help her mother at the bakery, but she's too young to do anything until her mother needs an emergency cake delivery.

- *Homer Price* by Robert McCloskey (Puffin, 1976)
  A little boy has a run-in with a doughnut machine that will not turn off.

- *Mmm, Cookies!* by Robert Munsch (Cartwheel, 2002)
  Christopher bakes his parents a cookie out of play clay and presents it as a real cookie. His parents want to teach him a lesson, so they ask his teacher for help.

- *The Magic School Bus Gets Baked in a Cake: A Book about Kitchen Chemistry* by Joanna Cole (Scholastic Paperbacks, 1995)
  Children are trying to get a birthday cake for their teacher when the magic school bus shrinks.

- *Walter the Baker* by Eric Carle (Aladdin, 1998)
  This is the story of a baker who invented the pretzel.

Storage Container

A large box decorated with pictures of baked goods can be suitable to hold all of the props and materials for this center.

      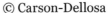

Implementing the Bakery

Procedures:

Step 1   Visit a local bakery to see how it is set up and to observe the various types of literacy materials that are displayed. Ask the store manager for various-sized boxes for baked goods, bread bags, hats, white paper bags, and napkins.

Step 2   Collect or create as many props, print, and writing materials as possible from the props and materials lists. Create a storage container by attaching recipes and pictures of baked goods to a large box or plastic bin. Visit the local library to check out books. Be sure to get some fiction books and some cookbooks. Locate recipes for making doughnuts, bread, muffins, cookies, or cake and copy it with rebus pictures on chart paper.

Step 3   Gather the cooking pans, utensils, and ingredients. Make or purchase a variety of colorful play dough to be used in all recipes. Download appropriate environmental print and signs from the Internet. Create a rebus menu. Prepare a chart titled "Shapes of Bread" divided into two sections labeled "Shaped Like a Circle," and "Not Shaped Like a Circle." Copy the song, "Little Doughnuts" (page 117) and/or "The Muffin Man" (page 117) on chart paper. Cut a doughnut with a hole in the middle out of card stock. This doughnut will be used with the song "Little Doughnuts." Cut out a hole in the dough- nut large enough for the word **doughnuts** to show through when the paper doughnut is placed over the song lyrics.

Little Doughnuts
(to the tune of "Ten Little Indians")
One lit...   three little doughnuts
Fo...   ...ix little doughnuts
Sev... ...ie, eight l...   ...ne little doughnuts
doughnuts   ...bakery shop.

Step 4   Ask the parents to send in their child's favorite bread, cookie, cupcake, muffin, or doughnut recipe. Invite children to share these recipes and then sort the recipes into categories. These recipes could be compiled and made into a recipe booklet.

Step 5   Choose an area in the classroom close to the Housekeeping center so children will have access to the stove, sink, and refrigerator. Display the charted recipe(s) for baked goods next to a table that has been covered with paper. Place the ingredients and baking supplies on the table. Hang an apron and a baker's hat close to this table. Provide an area for the cake decorator to ice the cookies or cupcakes or to glaze the doughnuts. Place the deep fryer and the timer on the stove. Set up a counter area using a table and place the cash register and bill forms here. Hang the sign for the baked goods and their prices behind the counter. Place the Daily Specials board next to the cash register. Place the plastic trays that will be used to display the baked goods on a bookcase or other shelving unit. Set up the drink stand on another table by placing the cups next to the coffee pot and hot cocoa pot in an area accessible to the customers. Use another table with chairs for the customers.

Step 6 Provide time for children to use environmental print to design bakery place mats. See Bauer, Walcavich, and Nipps (2006) for directions to create place mats. If possible, laminate the place mats for durability.

Step 7 Gather children in the reading area and tell them that they will have a special snack today. It is shaped like a circle, has a hole in the middle, and begins with **D**. Lead them to guess that it is a doughnut and then show them the word cards for **doughnut** and **circle**. Stress the beginning sound/letter of each word and ask for a volunteer to place the words on the word wall. Sing the "Little Doughnuts" song with children.

> **Little Doughnuts**
> (to the tune of "Ten Little Indians")
>
> One little, two little, three little doughnuts
> Four little, five little, six little doughnuts
> Seven little, eight little, nine little doughnuts
> Ten doughnuts in the bakery shop.

Show children the large paper doughnut and ask for a volunteer to place it on the chart so that the word **doughnuts** shows through the hole. Choose another volunteer and sing the song again. Enjoy the doughnut for snack time, and while children are eating them, ask if they know how doughnuts are made. Share the recipe and talk about the different kinds of doughnuts. Show them the menu and tell them that soon there will be a new literacy play center called the Bakery. Instead of doughnuts, you may want to have muffins and sing "The Muffin Man" song.

> **The Muffin Man**
>
> Oh, do you know the muffin man,
> The muffin man, the muffin man?
> Oh, do you know the muffin man,
> Who lives on Drury Lane.
>
> Yes, I know the muffin man,
> The muffin man, the muffin man.
> Yes, I know the muffin man,
> Who lives on Drury Lane.

Step 8 Lead children to the Bakery. Show them the sign and ask for a volunteer to read the name of the Bakery. Show them the area where the baker will make the various baked goods and ask for a volunteer to play this role. Read the charted rebus recipe aloud and gather the materials and ingredients as they are needed in the recipe.

Direct the baker to put on the hat and apron and follow each step of the recipe. Demonstrate how to roll out the play dough to make the baked product. Set the timer so that children will know how long to bake it. Choose another volunteer to be the cake decorator. Have this person decorate the baked product. For example, paper confetti could be used for sprinkles. Tell them that baked goods are sold individually, as a half dozen, or a dozen. Ask for a volunteer to count out 6 items and put them in a box. Tell children that 6 items is a half dozen. Ask another volunteer to count out 12 items and place them in a box. Explain that 12 items makes a dozen. Direct children to look at the sign showing the price of baked goods. Ask them to find the picture with 6 items. Demonstrate how to read the sign to determine how much a half dozen items cost. Model how to write the cost on a price tag and attach it to the box. Repeat this procedure to find the cost of a dozen items.

Show children how the baked goods will be displayed. Individual items will be on trays behind the counter. Customers must ask the salesclerk to get the baked goods they want. Other baked goods will be in boxes or bags on shelves. Customers will take these items from the shelf and pay for them at the cash register.

Some bakeries also sell drinks. Show children the drink counter with the cocoa machine, coffee pot, and cups. Model how the customer will fill a cup with a beverage and pay for it at the cash register.

Step 9 Gather children into the reading area and read the book, *Bread, Bread, Bread* by Ann Morris (HarperTrophy, 1993). Point out how many different types of bread there are in the world. You may want to ask parents to send in one of the types of bread mentioned in the book so children could sample it. Suggested types include pita bread, bagels, tortilla shells, raisin bread, pumpernickel, French bread, and whole grain. Point out the different shapes of these breads. Children could classify the breads by placing a picture of each bread on the "Types of Bread" chart that was previously created.

Step 10 Prior to opening the Bakery, review the rules that are posted in the classroom. Show them the chart with the roles that they can play at this center. Encourage children to count how many children can play in this center at one time. Remind them that this center will be open for three to four weeks so everyone will have a chance to play in the Bakery. Review all of the word cards for this center.

Step 11 Gather the assessment materials that will be used in this center and place them in a convenient location near the Bakery. Any of the assessment instruments would be appropriate for this center.

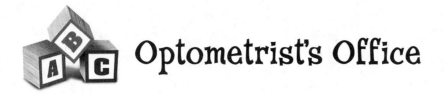

Optometrist's Office

Goals and Objectives for Children

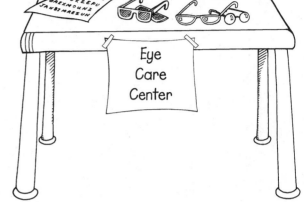

1. To develop an understanding of how an optometrist's office operates through practice and simulation

2. To practice oral communication skills through role-playing various roles, such as optometrist, receptionist, optometrist's assistant, office assistant, and patient

3. To practice oral communication skills by greeting patients, talking to the patients and optometrist, fitting glasses, and purchasing glasses

4. To develop concepts of print by reading environmental print, pamphlets, charts, magazines, and center books (page 121)

5. To refine book-handling skills by reading the various books and magazines in the center

6. To reinforce phonemic awareness and letter recognition of the **O** sound in **optometrist**, the **P** sound in **patient**, the **G** sound in **glasses** and **green**, the **F** sound in **frames**, the **B** sound in **brown** and **blue**, the **H** sound in **hazel**, the **U** sound in **up**, and the **D** sound in **down**

7. To identify letters of the alphabet by reading an eye chart

8. To practice reading skills by reading environmental print and patient charts

9. To practice writing skills by completing customers' orders, bills, and receipts

10. To practice counting to 11 by counting the letters in **optometrist**

11. To practice recognizing numerals by reading numbers during the eye exam

12. To identify colors by naming them during the eye exam

13. To develop positional awareness and directionality by pointing in the correct direction during the eye exam (as directed by the eye chart)

14. To develop cooperative learning skills by interacting with other children at the Optometrist's Office

Props

- Mirrors—hand and table
- Magnifying glasses
- Old glasses
- Sunglasses with lenses
- Sunglasses without lenses
- Small plastic rulers
- Cash register
- Play money
- Empty eye-drop bottles

- Lab coats
- Pictures of people wearing glasses
- Cases for glasses
- Wooden spoon (for covering an eye during eye exam)
- Trays for glasses
- Flashlight without batteries
- Stool
- Play debit/credit cards

Print Materials

- Center sign with name of the Optometrist's Office
- Insurance cards
- Literature and pamphlets on eyes and eye care
- Signs for Open/Closed, Exit, Hours of Operation, No Smoking, Check-In Here, Check-Out Here, Exam Room
- Appointment book
- Magazines for waiting area
- Name tags
- Folders and charts for patients
- Labels for doctor's tools
- Eye charts
- Poster of an eye
- Pictures of eyes

- Calendar
- Business cards
- "My Glasses" (page 122) written on chart paper
- Eye exam book with numbers in different colors
- Bills, receipts, and charge slips
- Chart with pictures of the roles children can play in this center, including doctor, doctor's assistant, receptionist, office assistant, and patient
- Graph with title "Our Eye Colors" on chart paper
- Rebus word cards for **B–brown**, **B–blue**, **G–green**, **H–hazel**, **P–patient**, **G–glasses**, **F–frames**, **U–up**, **D–down**

Writing Materials

- Pens, pencils, and markers
- Sign-in book
- Patient charts
- Insurance forms
- Office billing statement
- Prescription pads

- Folders
- Bills/receipts/charge slips
- Checks
- Appointment book
- Appointment cards
- Name cards

Book List

- *Arthur's Eyes* by Marc Brown (Little, Brown and Co., 1986)
  After getting glasses, Arthur's classmates tease him. Arthur stops wearing glasses, but finds it's OK to be different.

- *Glasses for D. W.* by Marc Brown (Random House Books for Young Readers, 1996)
  Arthur's sister, D. W., wants to wear glasses just like her big brother.

- *Glasses (Who Needs 'Em?)* by Lane Smith (Puffin, 1995)
  An optometrist tries to convince his young patient to wear glasses.

- *I Need Glasses: My Visit to the Optometrist* by Virginia Dooley (Mondo Publishing, 2002)
  The story describes a visit to the optometrist.

- *Luna and the Big Blur: A Story for Children Who Wear Glasses* by Shirley Day (Magination Press, 2000)
  Luna hates her glasses until Daddy helps her see all of the wonderful things that are special about her.

- *Magenta Gets Glasses* by Deborah Reber (Simon Spotlight/Nickelodeon, 2002)
  Magenta goes to the eye doctor for glasses. She has an eye exam, picks out purple frames, and gets her glasses fitted.

Storage Container

Decorate a box or plastic bin with pictures of people wearing glasses. Posters and charts can have two or three holes punched in them and can be hung from hooks in the classroom or on a chart stand.

      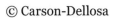

Implementing the Optometrist's Office

Procedures:

Step 1   Visit local optometrists to collect sample brochures, pamphlets, and any items the office can donate. Observe the surroundings carefully to see how the office and waiting room are set up and to note the way frames are displayed. Observe the literature that is available and the signs that are posted.

Step 2   Collect or create as many props, print, and writing materials as possible from the props and materials lists. Visit the local library to check out books. Be sure to get some nonfiction books on optometrists and eyes.

Step 3   Download appropriate environmental print and images from the Internet. Create an E–eye chart (officially called an illiterate eye chart) and a letter–eye chart (officially known as a Snellen eye chart). Samples of eye charts can be found on the Internet by typing "Snellen eye chart" in the search window. Using the sample eye chart, write the letters on a large sheet of poster board or print letters using different-size fonts and glue them on a large sheet of poster board. Create a chart that has a simple illustration of parts of the eye by downloading and printing images from the Internet. Make a book to identify colors by cutting white construction paper into 6" x 6" (15.24 cm x 15.24 cm) squares. Write a dotted number on each page using different colorful markers or arrange sticker dots of different colors to make a number on each page. Write the word **Colors** on the front of the book and staple the pages together.

My Glasses

My glasses help me see
Clearly as can be.
I can see up and down
And all around the town.

Write the poem "My Glasses" on chart paper. Remember to leave space between the lines. Create the patient folders, patient charts, name tags, appointment book, sign-in pad, prescription pad, signs, and other print materials.

Step 4 Choose an area in the classroom to set up the Optometrist's Office. Create a waiting area with a table for the receptionist. Place a telephone, appointment book, patient folders, and charts on the receptionist's table. In the doctor's office, place a chair for the patient, a stool for the doctor, and a small table for the exam instruments. Put the eye-exam charts and illustrations of the parts of an eye on the wall. Set up a section for patients to choose glasses. Put glasses on trays and display them on a table. Place table mirrors on the display table for patients to look at themselves as they try on glasses. Place pictures of people wearing glasses in this area. Hang all of the signs and label the props. Place the lab coats in the doctor's office.

Step 5 Introduce the center by gathering children together in the circle area. Show children the mirrors and pass them out. Ask children to look at their eyes in the mirrors and decide what color eyes they have. Help them as necessary to decide on their eye color. Pass out squares of paper on which a picture of an eye has been drawn. Ask children to go back to their tables to color the eye to match their eye color. When everyone is finished, ask children to bring their paper to the circle area. Show children the graph labeled "Our Eye Colors." Read the title of the graph with children. Point to the bottom of the graph and help children read the colors brown, blue, green, and hazel. Ask children who have brown eyes to stand. One at a time, ask them to bring their paper to the chart. Attach each paper to the chart above the correct color. Repeat with the other colors. Once the graph is completed, discuss the results with children. Children can identify the most and least common eye color. They can compare two eye colors to determine which occurs most or least.

After discussing the graph, ask children to read the colors again. Show them the word cards for each color and have children match the word cards to the words on the graph. Place the words on the word wall. Play I Spy with children. Make sure children include the color of the object they spy. For example, "I spy with my little eye, something yellow, and I use it when I write."

Step 6 Ask children what some people wear to help them see more clearly. Show the word card for **glasses**. Read the word and ask children to identify the beginning letter in glasses. Have children make the sound for **G** and ask for other words that start with **G**. Place the word on the word wall and read the other **G** words.

Tell children that today they are going to participate in an activity to show them what it is like when someone isn't able to see clearly. Explain that while glasses usually help people see more clearly, they are going to put on special glasses that will make things blurry. Tell them they will look at a picture through the special glasses and try to decide what it is. Ask for three or four volunteers. Give each child a pair of sunglasses on which Vaseline® has been rubbed on the lenses. Show the class the picture and stress that they are not to say aloud what they see. Then, show children with the glasses the picture. Ask them to identify what they see. Have them remove the glasses and look at the picture. Discuss whether they were correct and ask how the picture looks different without the glasses. Repeat the activity using different pictures until everyone has had a chance to try the glasses. Tell children that if their vision is blurry, they need to tell their parents so that they can have their eyes checked.

Read the poem, "My Glasses" (page 122). Ask a child to identify the rhyming words.

Step 7 Ask if anyone has ever been to an eye doctor. Tell them one kind of an eye doctor is called an optometrist. Write the word **optometrist** on the board and have children read the word. Tell them **optometrist** is a really big word and have them count the number of letters it has. Ask what letter **optometrist** starts with and have children make that sound for **O**. Have children say **optometrist** and clap out the syllables.

If children have been to an optometrist, ask them to share what happened. Remind children of the experiment with the blurry glasses. Tell them that an optometrist checks their vision to determine if they can see clearly.

Tell children that the optometrist uses special eye charts to check their vision. Show them the E–eye chart and have them identify the letter **E**. Point to the largest **E** on the chart and ask children to point in the direction the three lines are facing. Point to other **E**s on the chart and have children point in the direction the lines are facing. As children point in the direction the lines

are facing, they may identify the direction with the words up, down, and to the side. Show children the word cards for **up** and **down**, read them aloud, and ask what letter is at the beginning of each word. Have children make the beginning sounds and place the word cards on the word wall.

Ask children what happens to the size of the **E**s on the chart. Explain why the letters become smaller. Tell children that this is one of the ways an optometrist checks their vision and that this eye chart will be in the Optometrist's Office for them to use.

Step 8 Show children an eye chart with different letters on it. Remind them of the E-eye chart that they used previously. Explain that sometimes an optometrist will use a letter-eye chart. Point to the different letters on the chart and ask children to name them. Again point out how the letters become smaller on the chart. Tell children this eye chart will be in the Optometrist's Office for them to use.

 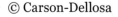

Step 9 Gather children together. Read and discuss one of the books about optometrists with children. Show them pictures of optometrist's offices. Point out the display cases with the different frames for glasses. Show children the word card for **frames**. Ask a child to identify the beginning letter. Have children make the sound for **F**, place the word frames on the word wall and read the words that start with **F**. If there are children in the group who wear glasses, ask them to come to the front, one at a time. Point out the color and shape of the frame. Tell children there are many different kinds of frames to choose from when they go to the optometrist. Show children a tray on which different glasses have been placed. Discuss the different colors and shapes of the frames.

Step 10 Show children the sign for the Optometrist's Office. Have them come into the office. Explain that the office has three areas. The first area is the check-in and waiting room. Model how to sign-in for an appointment. Show them the magazines, books, and other literature to read while waiting for the doctor. Ask for a volunteer to be the patient and model how the receptionist greets the patient. Demonstrate how the receptionist writes the patient's name on the folder and puts the patient's chart inside the folder.

The second area is the doctor's office. Demonstrate how a doctor's assistant calls the patient to come into the office and shows the patient where to sit for the examination. Have the patient sit in the examination chair. Open the folder and write the patient's name on the chart. Tell the patient the doctor will be right in.

Ask a child to be the doctor's assistant. Have the child put on a lab coat. Model how the doctor and his/her assistant conduct an eye examination. Put on the doctor's coat, walk into the office with the assistant, and greet the patient. Have the assistant give the patient the book of colors. Explain that optometrists check for color deficiency by having patients read numbers in a special book. Ask the patient to read the numbers and identify their colors. Record the results on the patient's chart. Ask the patient to look at the E-eye chart on the wall. Ask the assistant to give the patient the wooden spoon. Ask the patient to carefully cover one eye with the spoon. Have the assistant point to the first **E** on the chart. Ask the patient to point in the direction the three lines of the **E** are facing. Have the assistant point to several other **E**s and, each time, ask the patient to indicate where the three lines are facing. Ask the patient to move the wooden spoon to the other eye and repeat the procedure. Record the results on the patient's chart. Pretend to put drops in the patient's eyes. Then, ask the patient to look at the letter chart. Conduct an eye examination as before but have the patient identify letters. Using the small flashlight (without batteries) and the magnifying glass, pretend to peer into the patient's eyes. Stress that the

     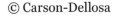

optometrist is careful not to touch the eyes with the dropper or the light. Write a prescription for the glasses. Ask the assistant to show the patient into the eyeglass-fitting room.

The third area is the eyeglass-fitting room for selecting frames and having the glasses adjusted to fit. The check-out desk, where customers pay for the doctor's visit and glasses, is also located here. Show children the display of frames and the Frames sign. Have children read the sign and find the word on the word wall. Explain that patients choose the frames they like for the lenses to be placed in to make the glasses. Select a child to try on different frames and model how the office assistant helps the patient choose frames. Use the small ruler to measure the bridge of the nose to help fit the frames. Have the patient select a case for the glasses and pay for the glasses at the check-out desk with cash or credit.

Step 11   Before opening the Optometrist's Office, review the rules that are posted in the classroom. Remind children to sign the role chart and create a name tag. Tell them how many children can play in the center at one time and that the center will be open for three to four weeks so that everyone will have an opportunity to assume the different roles. Review all of the word wall cards for this center. Show children the various books that have been placed in the center and encourage them to read these books while this center is open.

Step 12   Collect the assessment materials that will be used in this center and place them in a convenient location. Any of the assessment instruments may be used with this center.

 Movie Theater

Goals and Objectives for Children

1. To develop an understanding of how a movie theater operates through practice and simulation

2. To develop oral communication skills through role-playing various roles, such as usher, concession stand worker, manager, cashier, ticket taker, movie critic, and moviegoer

3. To develop oral communication skills by talking with customers, selling tickets, and selling concessions

4. To develop concepts of print by reading movie posters and center books (page 129)

5. To reinforce book-handling skills by reading the various books at the center

6. To reinforce phonemic awareness and letter recognition of the **M** sound in **movie**, the **P** sound in **popcorn**, **pop**, and **pot**, the **T** sound in **ticket**, the **U** sound in **usher**, and the **C** sound in **candy**

7. To introduce phonemic awareness and letter recognition of the ending **P** sound in **pop** and the ending **T** sound in **pot**

8. To develop reading skills by reading environmental print, ticket stubs, and movie reviews

9. To develop reading skills by identifying the literary elements of a story—the characters, setting, main events, problem, and solution—by recalling what happened in the beginning, middle, and end of a movie

10. To develop writing skills by creating name tags, designing movie posters, and creating tickets for the movies

11. To develop writing skills by writing movie reviews and rating the movies

12. To develop math skills by working with money, pricing candy, and rating movies

13. To develop cooperative learning skills by interacting with other children in the Movie Theater

     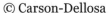

Props

- Ticket window
- Movie tickets
- Cash register
- Play money and Play debit/credit cards
- Flashlight for usher
- Numbered pillows or chairs for seating
- Movie screen or large sheet
- Children's movies

- Popcorn machine
- Popcorn boxes or bags
- Drink cups
- Empty candy boxes
- Napkins
- Videos or DVDs
- VCR or DVD player
- Large yellow stars to rank the movies

Print Materials

- Center sign with the name of the Movie Theater
- Movie posters
- Theater marquee
- Price list for tickets
- Menu and price list for concession stand
- Signs for Open/Closed, Exit, Hours of Operation, No Smoking, Quiet Please
- Name tags for workers

- Newspaper ads about movies
- Chart with pictures of the roles children can play in this center, including usher, concession stand worker, manager, cashier, ticket taker, and moviegoer
- Rebus word cards for **M–movie**, **U–usher**, **T–ticket**, **P–popcorn**, **P–pop**, **P–pot**, **C–candy**
- "The Popcorn Song" (page 130) written on chart paper

Writing Materials

- Name tags
- Movie review forms
- Pens, pencils, and markers
- Blank tickets

- Adding machine tape that children can use to draw and write their own movie
- Labels for pricing the candy

Book List

- *If You Take a Mouse to the Movies* by Laura Numeroff (Laura Geringer, 2000)
  If you take a mouse to the movies, he will ask for popcorn and . . . . This cumulative story will delight your children.

- *Curious George Goes to a Movie* by H. A. Rey (Houghton Mifflin, 1998)
  George promises to be good at the movies, but he gets curious! Of course this leads to another exciting adventure for George and the man with the yellow hat.

- *The Popcorn Book* by Tomie DePaola (Holiday House, 1984)
  While children make popcorn, the history of popcorn is told.

- *Who's at the Movies?* by Yukiko Kido (Sterling Press, 2006)
  It's movie time for Nomi and her friends.

Storage Container

A large box decorated with empty VCR tapes or DVDs could be used to store the props and materials.

Implementing the Movie Theater

Procedures:

Step 1   Visit local movie theaters to observe how the ticket booth, concession area, projection room, and theater are set up. Note the different types of literacy materials that are displayed (marquees, posters, notice of coming attractions, ticket price list, and concession price list). You may want to set up time to speak with the manager to see if the theater has old posters or signs that they may want to share. Scan the newspapers and the Internet for movie ads that can be adapted to use in this literacy play center.

Step 2   Collect or create as many props, print, and writing materials as possible from the props and materials lists. Visit the local library to check out a variety of books about movies as well as books that have been made into movies.

Step 3   Collect VCR tapes and DVD cases that can be attached to the large box for the storage container to pique children's interest. Download appropriate environmental print that can be used to design the movie signs, tickets, and concession stand supplies. Attach posters or pictures of movie characters to the outside of the box with Velcro® so that children can use them later in the center.

 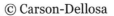

Step 4 Introduce this center by making popcorn for children to have for snack time. Share "The Popcorn Song" with children. While they are eating the popcorn, ask them when they usually eat popcorn. Lead them to mention movies and engage them in a conversation about movies by asking for volunteers to describe the last movie that they saw. Feel free to prompt them by showing the storage container that has been designed for this center and inviting them to identify the movies depicted by the VCR and DVD cases. Encourage them to talk about the characters that were in each movie, the setting, and something about the beginning, middle, and end of the movie. Ask them to discuss the problem that was in the movie and how it was solved. This will help them to develop a sense of story while identifying the literary elements.

> The Popcorn Song
>
> Popcorn kernels, popcorn kernels
>
> In the pot, in the pot.
>
> Shake them, shake them, shake them,
>
> Shake them, shake them, shake them,
>
> 'Til they POP, 'til they POP!

Depending on children's interests, you may want to make a story map of a movie that several children are familiar with by constructing a chart with five circles that have been labeled Characters, Setting, Events, Problem, and Solution. Draw the elements as they are discussed. Encourage children to retell the story of the movie using the story map.

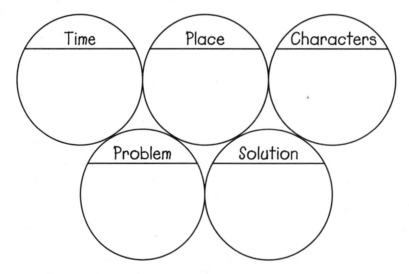

Step 5 Allow children to play a key role in designing the props for this center. Show them the large poster board and ask for suggestions on what to call their movie theater. Record their suggestions so that they can vote on their favorite title. Circle the winning name and identify each letter so children can use that for a model when they are designing their ticket stubs. Ask them

© Carson-Dellosa

where they would like to set up their new Movie Theater center. Show them the various props in the box that have been collected and put children into groups to work on the materials. One group could design the ticket stubs on colorful paper by copying the name of the theater on the top part of the ticket. Another group could create the concession stand menu by pasting the matching environmental print next to the items that they think should be on sale. They can also set up the concession stand by arranging the popcorn maker, popcorn boxes, drink stand with cups and straws, and pricing the candy boxes. Some children could be in charge of numbering the pillows or chairs for the theater. Others could decide what posters to hang and where they should be located. Other children could draw the characters that can be role-played in this center by referring to a chart with the names of the roles written on it. Allow sufficient work time so that children can accomplish all of these tasks. Children can also be encouraged to make their own movie by drawing scenes from their favorite movie or book on adding-machine paper. Offer help as needed.

Step 6   Gather children in the area that has been designated as the Movie Theater. Share completed props and materials. Sing "The Popcorn Song" again and show them the word cards for **popcorn**, **pop**, and **pot**. Ask for a volunteer to match these cards to the words in the song. Point out the words **pop** and **pot** and ask children to name the letters in both words. Ask them how the two words differ and underline the ending letter. Point out how changing just one letter can make a whole new word. Add all three **P** words to the word wall and read all of the words under the letter **P**. Show them the word cards for **movie**, **usher**, **ticket**, and **candy**. Have children read the words aloud, stressing the beginning sound. Relate each word to the new literacy play center by showing the corresponding prop/material. Ask for volunteers to place the words on the word wall. Read all of the words that begin with these letters/sounds on the word wall.

Step 7   Share a book from the list and review the elements of a story with children. Create a story map of the literary elements. Show them the other books that will be read while their new center is open.

Step 8   Read the sign with the name that they have chosen for the Movie Theater. Point out the different roles that they can play in the Movie Theater by reading them from the chart that has been posted. Tell them that because this is a Movie Theater, more children can play at one time in this center. Show children the numbered cushions or chairs where the moviegoers can sit and help them to count how many children can view the movie at the same time. Point out the other designated areas in the theater, such as the concession stand, the ticket window, the projection booth, and the manager's office. (Be sure to label each area.) Ask them to recall what moviegoers do first when they arrive at a theater. Walk them through the steps: 1) read the ads to see what is playing and what time it starts, 2) buy a ticket, 3) stop at the concession stand to buy popcorn, a drink, and candy, 4) hand their ticket to the usher, 5) decide where to sit in the theater, and 6) enjoy the movie. This sequence could be written on a chart so children can refer to it while playing in this center. Demonstrate each step by asking for volunteers to play each role and leading them through the steps. Tell all participants to make their own name tags.

Model how the ticket taker tears the ticket in half, keeping one part and returning the stub to the moviegoer. Turn the concession sign to Open, read the price list aloud with children, and ask a child to place an order. Demonstrate how to greet the customer, make the customer's order by placing the popcorn in the popcorn box, filling the drink order, and handing the customer the candy that was ordered. Read the price of each item from the concession stand menu and enter those numbers in the cash register. Count the money that the child pays with and give him change. Remind them that people should always show good manners and model this by thanking the customer. Instruct the child who is role-playing the manager that it her responsibility to greet the moviegoers and tell them to "Enjoy the show." Tell the child who wants to be the usher how to use the flashlight to direct the moviegoers to their seats. Hand children who have chosen to be movie critics the movie-rating form that either you or the children have designed. Tell them that their job is to carefully watch the movie and award it four stars if they really liked it, three stars if they thought it was good, two stars if they thought it was OK, one star if they didn't enjoy it, and zero stars if they thought it was really bad. After children are seated, have the projectionist place the video (or DVD) in the player.

Step 9   After the movie is over, ask the critics to share their review by telling everyone how many stars they awarded it. Gather children in the reading area and ask them to help write a review of the movie by sharing what they liked and disliked. Write this review on chart paper and reread it with children. Have large stars available so children can add them to the printed review.

Step 10   Gather the assessment materials that will be used in this center and place them in a convenient location near the Movie Theater. You will use the Oral Retelling Assessment (page 151).

 # Assessment of Children's Skills

The Importance of Assessment

Assessment should be an ongoing, integral component of any early childhood program. With the growing diversity in today's programs, it is increasingly important to be knowledgeable about children in their classrooms. Assessment helps determine children's development and skills at a particular point in time and tracks their progress and change (McAfee and Leong, 2002). Because young children's development and skills continually change, it is important to systematically assess children throughout the year.

Ongoing assessment involves gathering information during everyday class activities (Dodge, Heroman, Charles, and Maiorca, 2004). Such assessment provides a representative picture of children's knowledge and skills. Information from assessment allows you to find out what children are thinking, doing, and learning.

Assessment practices include observing and documenting what children say and do, collecting samples of children's work, interacting with children to listen to their conversations, and working with individual children on meaningful assessment tasks. In the early childhood program, assessment should be imbedded in the curriculum and/or emerge from the goals that the program strives to help children accomplish.

The key to observation is to observe purposefully and document examples that provide useful data (Dodge, Heroman, Charles, and Maiorca, 2004). You must be familiar with the program goals and objectives in order to observe purposefully. Observation requires you to objectively view and record children's behavior while they are engaged in activities within the program. You can use this information to determine children's progress toward goals and objectives.

Interacting with children while they play offers an opportunity to obtain rich data about their thinking, language, and skills. It allows you to build a relationship with every child, to understand their strengths, and to decide how to support their growth.

Children will be at different levels of development and will exhibit a range of skills. Working with individual children on specific assessment tasks related to the ongoing activities and learning in the classroom allows you to gain a deeper understanding of each child's development and skills.

After obtaining data about individual children, determine their progress toward the goals and objectives of the program. Progress can be viewed as a continuum where children are moving toward being more proficient in using the skills the program seeks to develop. Assessment enables you to reflect on children in your program. The results of assessment provide information to support children's learning and to plan meaningful curriculum for children (Dodge, Heroman, Charles, and Maiorca, 2004). You can make adjustments to the curriculum and adapt your instruction to meet the individual needs of each child.

Frequency of Assessing Skills

A system of ongoing assessment linked to goals and objectives helps ensure children will make progress. You can answer the following questions: 1) What do children know and what can they do? 2) How can I adjust the curriculum to meet their needs? and 3) How do I adapt my instruction? The assessment instruments provided in this book are designed to assess young children's literacy development, number and shape recognition, and socialization skills. For each literacy play center, several assessment instruments have been suggested. Decide which assessment instruments to utilize with each center based on children's needs.

During the time the center is available, observe and interact with children. Information needed to complete many of the assessment instruments can be obtained while children are engaged in the centers and during small and large group times. Record observations by taking notes on children's behaviors and skills as they play. Assessing a few children each day will allow ample opportunity to gather data. You can also assess children individually in a brief amount of time using the assessment instruments provided.

Information from these assessment instruments will allow you to provide children with additional meaningful experiences to enhance their development and acquisition of skills.

Book-Handling Checklist

Date _____ Child's Name _____

Evaluator _____

Directions: Based on assessment results, check the appropriate column for the child's literacy stage.

U = Unobserved (Child does not demonstrate the skill with or without adult prompts.)

D = Developing (Child attempts the skill with adult prompts.)

A = Achieved (Child demonstrates the skill independently.)

Book Orientation	U	D	A
Holds book right side up			
Identifies top/bottom of book			
Recognizes front/back of book			
Turns pages from front to back of book			
Turns pages one at a time			
Book Awareness	U	D	A
Tells story while turning pages			
Uses pictures to "read" the story			
Identifies the title of the book			
Identifies the author of the book			
Identifies the illustrator of the book			
Text Awareness	U	D	A
Recognizes words not picture are read (or child points to the words while telling the story)			
Recognizes pages are read from top to bottom			
Recognizes pages are read from left to right			
Sweeps from end of line to beginning of next line			
Can point to a letter			
Can point to a word			
Can point to the beginning letter of a word			
Can point to the ending letter of a word			

Oral Language Rating Scale

Date _____ Child's Name _____

Evaluator _____

Directions: Rate the child's level of performance in each category by placing an X in the appropriate box.

Expressive Language

	Always	Usually	Seldom	Never
Uses complete sentences				
Uses 5–6 word sentences				
Uses correct word order in sentences				
Asks questions with proper word order				
Uses past-tense verbs correctly				
Makes "No" responses with proper word order				
Uses vocabulary appropriate to the topic				
Uses descriptive words in sentences				
Contributes to conversations with other children				
Speaks clearly enough to be understood by others				
Uses appropriate volume when speaking				
Speaks with expression				

Receptive Language

	Always	Usually	Seldom	Never
Points to common pictures or objects when asked				
Listens and responds to a story				
Listens and responds to others' conversations				
Follows two-step directions				
Repeats phrases and sentences				
Joins in choral readings of poems, songs, and finger plays				
Responds to questions effectively				
Listens and responds to group discussions				

Socialization Skills Rating Scale

Date _____ Child's Name _____

Evaluator _____

Directions: Rate the child's level of performance in each category by placing an X in the appropriate box.

	Always	Usually	Seldom	Never
Takes turns willingly				
Shares materials with others				
Makes appropriate choices				
Initiates play with others				
Listens to others				
Shows concern for others				
Expresses emotions in an appropriate manner				
Displays kindness to others				
Helps another to do a task				
Waits to take a turn				
Follows established rules				
Complies with request without a fuss				
Allows aggressive behavior to be redirected				
Expresses anger in words rather than actions				
Resolves play conflicts in a positive manner				

Alphabet Knowledge Assessment

Child's Name _____

Evaluator _____

Date _____   Score _____   Date _____   Score _____

Date _____   Score _____   Date _____   Score _____

Date _____   Score _____   Date _____   Score _____

Directions: Circle each letter that the child can name. Use a different color marker each time the assessment is administered.

B	F	L	P	M
T	S	K	H	E
D	N	C	I	X
Q	V	O	R	A
G	W	Z	J	Y
		U		

Shape Recognition Assessment

Child's Name _____

Evaluator _____

Date _____   Date _____   Date _____   Date _____

Directions: Use a different color pen for each assessment period. Circle the letter that denotes the child's ability to perform the task listed.

M = matching shape: Ask the child to point to the identical shapes in each line.

P = pointing to shape: Name the shape and ask the child to point to that shape.

N = naming shape: Point to the shape and ask the child to name it.

1.	Circle		**M**	**P**	**N**
2.	Triangle		**M**	**P**	**N**
3.	Square		**M**	**P**	**N**
4.	Rectangle		**M**	**P**	**N**
5.	Heart		**M**	**P**	**N**

Number Recognition Assessment

Child's Name _____

Evaluator _____

Date _____   Score _____   Date _____   Score _____

Date _____   Score _____   Date _____   Score _____

Date _____   Score _____   Date _____   Score _____

Directions: Circle each number that the child can name. Use a different color marker each time the assessment is administered.

3   7   5   8

11   6   10   2

9   4   0   12

1

Emergent and Early Writing Rubric

Date _____ Child's Name _____

Evaluator _____

Directions: Collect a sample of the child's writing. Compare the writing to the criteria below. Rate the child's level of performance on each writing sample by recording the date in the box next to the level demonstrated. Attach the writing sample to the rubric.

Rubric Samples		S1	S2	S3	S4
Random scribbles					
Uses scribbles for writing					
Uses directional scribbles (left to right) for writing					
Uses squiggles and marks as letters					
Uses letter forms randomly					
Writes identifiable letters, perhaps including own name					
Uses strings of letters (left to right, upper- and lowercase letters mixed)					
Uses groups of letters (letters with spaces to resemble words)					
Labels pictures (matching beginning sounds with letter printing)					
Writes own messages using invented/conventional spelling					

    © Carson-Dellosa

Rhyming Words Assessment

Introduce the assessment to children by saying, "I am going to say two words: cat . . . fat. These two words sound alike and are called rhyming words. Cat and fat have the same ending sound, so they rhyme.

"Now I am going to say two other words and I want you to listen to hear if they rhyme—**cat** . . . **mop**. These two words do not rhyme because they do not sound alike."

Show the child Sample Card A (page 144) and say, "Look at these pictures. I want you to listen while I name each picture." Direct the child to point to each picture as you name it. Then, have the child point to the picture on the bottom as you name it again. Tell the child to point to the picture that rhymes with hat (the bottom picture). Repeat the same procedure with Sample Card B (page 144).

Complete the assessment using the Rhyming Word Picture Cards (pages 144–146). Record the results on the Rhyming Words Assessment Form (page 143).

Syllable Recognition Assessment

Introduce the assessment to children by saying, "I am going to show you a picture. Listen carefully while I name the picture."

Show the child Sample Card A (page 148) and say, "This is a letter. Say the word with me—**letter**. **Letter** has two syllables. Say the word with me and clap each word part." (Repeat the word and clap the syllables with the child. Ask the child, "How many times did we clap?" Remind the child that you clapped two times because there are two syllables in the word **letter**.) Repeat the same procedures with Sample Card B (page 148).

Complete the assessment using the Syllable Recognition Picture Cards (pages 148–150). Record the results on the Syllable Recognition Assessment Form (page 147).

Rhyming Words Assessment Form

Date _____ Child's Name _____

Evaluator _____

Put an X in front of each pair of rhyming words the child correctly identifies.

_____ 1. rocks/socks

_____ 2. feet/meat   _____ 7. dish/fish

_____ 3. bat/cat   _____ 8. dog/frog

_____ 4. star/car   _____ 9. duck/truck

_____ 5. nose/rose   _____ 10. shell/bell

_____ 6. mail/nail

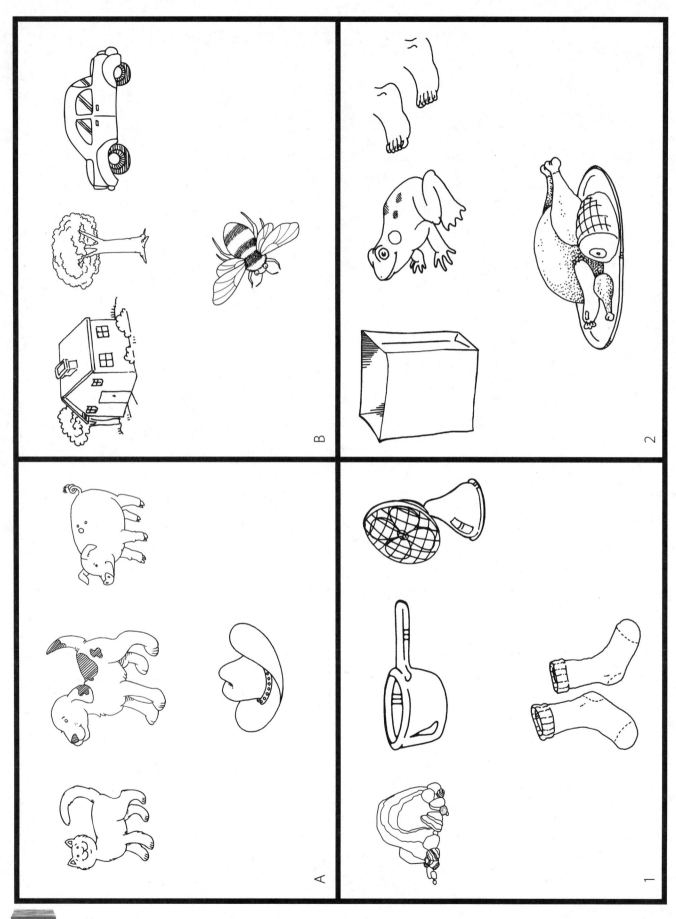

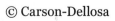

CD-104231 • Literacy Play Centers

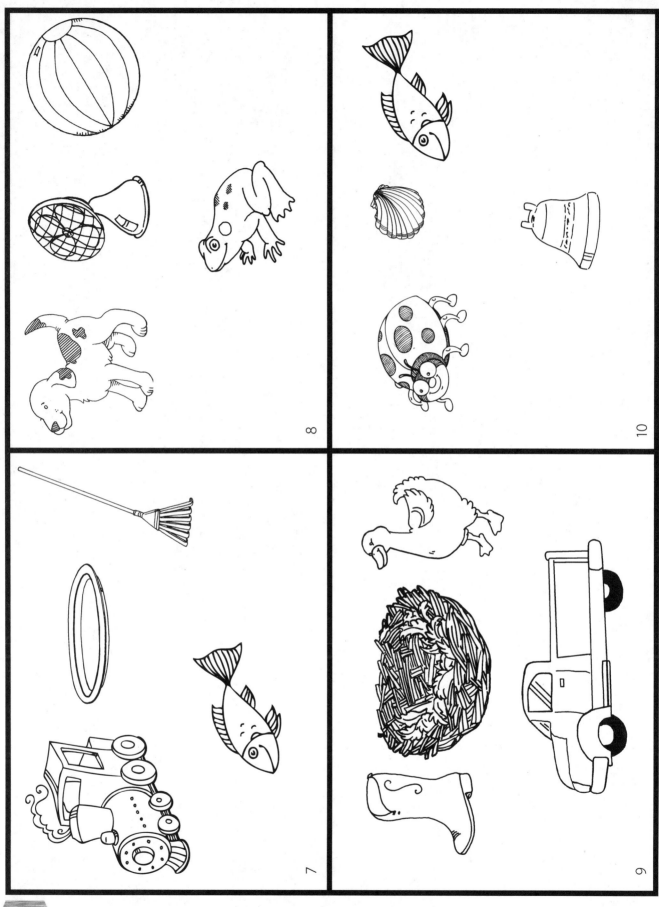

8

10

7

9

A E I O U

Syllable Recognition Assessment Form

Date _____ Child's Name _____

Evaluator _____

Put an X in front of words for which the child correctly identifies the number of syllables.

_____ 1. football   _____ 6. bat

_____ 2. kite   _____ 7. nickel

_____ 3. hammer   _____ 8. pot

_____ 4. shoe   _____ 9. pizza

_____ 5. umbrella   _____ 10. banana

     © Carson-Dellosa **147**

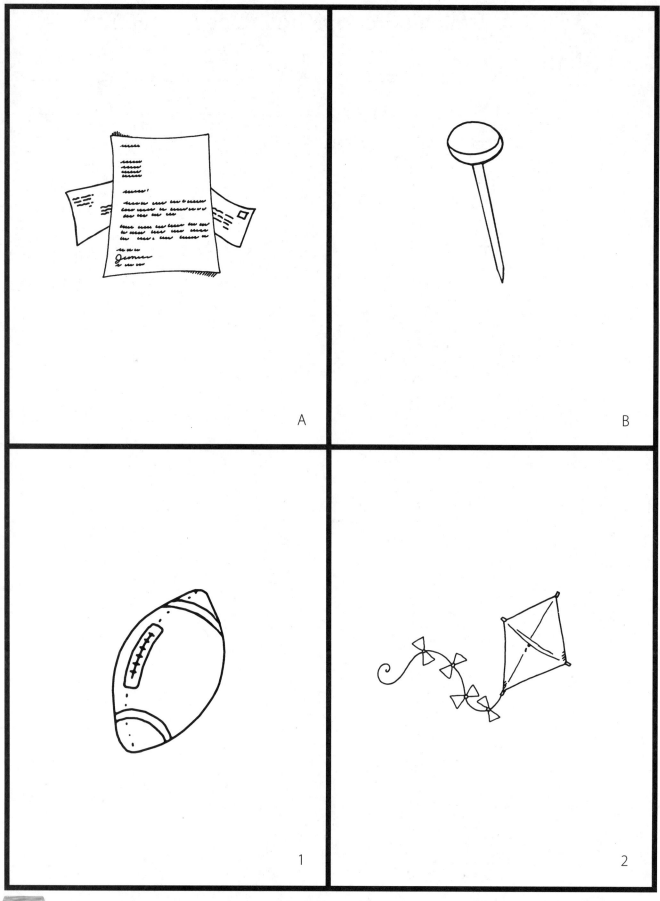

A

B

1

2

3

4

5

6

     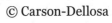

7

8

9

10

© Carson-Dellosa 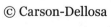   CD-104231 • Literacy Play Centers

Oral Retelling Assessment

Preparation

Begin by choosing a book that has a strong story structure and/or a character with whom children are familiar. Show the cover of the book to children. Involve children in a discussion about the cover by asking them to tell you about:

1) The picture

2) Who they see in the picture

3) Where they think the characters are

Elaborate on their answers. Show the cover again and take them on a picture walk through the story by pointing out important scenes. Ask children to listen carefully as you read the story aloud to find out who the characters are and what happens to them in the story. Tell them the character (little girl, bunny, etc.) in the story has a problem and they need to listen carefully to discover how the character solves the problem. Read the story without interruptions and show the pictures as you read.

Then, discuss the story by inviting children to name the main characters and any other important characters. Ask them to tell you what problem the main character had and how it was solved. Help children to figure out what happened in the beginning, middle, and end of the story. Then, go back to the front cover, review the name of the characters and identify the setting. Discuss the story with children.

Read the story at least two other times to children, or have them listen to the story on tape.

Conducting the Retelling

Conduct the retelling assessment with one child at a time. Ask each child to tell you about the story by using the following dialogue, "Yesterday, I read the story (name of book). I want you to tell me all about the story." If the child is hesitant to begin, show the book cover again and say "Once there was a . . . ," but do not give the book to the child. Record their answers on the recording sheet and check off what they include in their retelling. If the child needs help recalling the events, prompt by asking, "What came next?" or "How did the story end?"

After the child has retold the story, ask a question about the story to help the child make a personal connection.

Oral Retelling Assessment Form

Date _____   Child's Name _____

Evaluator _____

Title of Story _____ Author _____

Directions: Put an X next to each story element that the child includes in the retelling.

Setting

　Includes time or place _____

Characters

　Includes name of main character _____

　Describes main character _____

　Identifies other major characters _____

Problem

　Identifies major problem _____

Important Events

　Recalls major events _____

　Retells events in a correct sequence _____

Solution

　Tells how problem was solved _____

Connection

　Describes a personal connection with the text, which is _____

_____

Total Score _____ out of 9. Comments _____

_____

_____

Rebus Examples

Grocery List

☐ bananas

☐ milk

☐ bread

☐ orange juice

Fast-Food Restaurant Order Pad

☐ hamburger

☐ chicken sandwich

☐ french fries

☐ fruit cup

☐ drink(s)

Pizza Restaurant Menu

☐ pizza

   ☐ cheese

   ☐ pepperoni

☐ spaghetti

☐ salad

   ☐ drink(s)

Doctor's Office Symptoms Card

☐ cough

☐ runny nose

☐ tired

☐ stomach ache

Rebus Examples

Appointment Card

Name_____

Appointment on _____

☐ Mon   ☐ Tues   ☐ Wed   ☐ Thur   ☐ Fri

at

Flower Arrangements

☐   three flowers, small vase

☐   large bowl arrangement

☐   large vase arrangement

Dear Parents and Guardians,

This year literacy play centers will be incorporated into our curriculum. This means that an area in our classroom will be converted into a store, a shop, or a business similar to those that operate in our community. Possible centers include a grocery store, fast-food restaurant, post office, and a doctor's office. Opportunities for children to build their language, literacy skills, and math concepts will be integrated into the literacy play centers. As children interact with their friends, they will be able to play a variety of roles. Using the props and literacy materials in each center, children will be engaged in speaking, listening, reading, and writing.

Creating these centers will involve collecting a variety of materials that can easily be adapted to fit the theme of each center. I will need your help to amass these materials. Please begin now to save paper towel rolls, plastic trays, bags, empty cans, cardboard containers, and shoe boxes. I will also send a note home each month asking for specific materials to fit the theme of that month's literacy play center, which we will be creating.

I am currently developing our first literacy play center _____ .

For this center, please send in _____ , _____ ,

_____ , and _____ . The center

will be open _____ .

Thank you for your support,

References

Professional References

Antonacci, P. A. and C. M. O'Callaghan. 2005. *Portraits of literacy development: Instruction and assessment in a well-balanced literacy program, K–3*. Upper Saddle River, NJ: Prentice Hall.

Bauer, K., M. Walcavich, and L. Nipps. 2006. *Environmental print activities: Activities using logos, labels, packages, and signs*. Greensboro, NC: Carson-Dellosa.

Berk. L. 2005. *Child development*. 7th ed. Boston: Allyn and Bacon.

Cunningham, P. M. 2004. *Phonics they use: Words for reading and writing*. 4th ed. Boston: Allyn and Bacon.

Dodge, D. T., C. Heroman, J. Charles, and J. Maiorca. 2004. Beyond outcomes: How ongoing assessment supports children's learning and leads to meaningful curriculum. *Young Children* 59 (1): 20–28.

Frost, J. L. 1992. *Play and playscapes*. New York: Delmar Thomson Learning.

Kieff, J. E. and R. M. Casbergue. 1999. *Playful learning and teaching: Integrating play into preschool and primary programs*. Boston: Allyn and Bacon.

Levy, J. 1978. *Play behavior*. Melbourne, FL: Krieger Publishing.

McAfee, O., and D. J. Leong. 2002. *Assessing and guiding young children's development and learning*. 3rd ed. Boston: Allyn and Bacon.

Mitchell, L. 1934. *Young geographers*. New York: Bank Street College.

Morrow, L. 2001. *Literacy development in the early years: Helping children read and write*. 4th ed. Boston: Allyn and Bacon.

Raver, C. C. 2002. Emotions matter: Making the case for the role of young children's emotional development for early school readiness. *Social Policy Report* 16 (3).

Seefeldt, C. 2005. *Social studies for the preschool/primary child*. 7th ed. Upper Saddle River, NJ.: Prentice Hall.

Shore, R. 1997. *Rethinking the brain*. New York: Families and Work Institute.

Vygotsky, L. 1986. *Thought and language*. Cambridge, MA: The MIT Press.

Children's Works Cited

26 Letters and 99 Cents by Tana Hoban (HarperTrophy, 1995)

Aaron's Hair by Robert Munsch (Cartwheel, 2002)

Alexander Who Used to Be Rich Last Sunday by Judith Viorst (Aladdin, 1987)

Architecture Counts by Michael J. Crosbie and Steve Rosenthal (John Wiley and Sons, 1993)

Architecture Shapes by Michael J. Crosbie and Steve Rosenthal (John Wiley and Sons, 1993)

Arthur's Eyes by Marc Brown (Little, Brown and Co., 1986)

Arthur's Pet Business by Marc Brown (Little, Brown and Co., 1993)

B Is for Bulldozer: A Construction ABC by June Sobel (Gulliver Books, 2003)

Bank Tellers: Community Workers by Cynthia Klingel and Robert B. Noyed (Compass Point Books, 2002)

Baseball 1, 2, 3 by James Buckley (DK Publishing, 2001)

Baseball ABC by Florence Cassen Mayers (Harry N. Abrams, Inc., 1994)

Baseball A, B, C by James Buckley (DK Publishing, 2001)

The Baseball Counting Book by Barbara Barbieri McGrath (Charlesbridge, 1999)

The Baseball Star by Fred G. Arrigg, Jr. (Troll Communications, 1995)

Basketball A, B, C: The NBA Alphabet by Florence Cassen Mayers (Harry N. Abrams, Inc., 1996)

The Berenstain Bears Go to the Doctor by Stan and Jan Berenstain (Random House Books for Young Readers, 1981)

Biscuit by Alyssa Satin Capucilli (HarperTrophy, 1997)

Bob's Busy Year by Tricia Boczkowski (Simon Spotlight, 2003)

Bread, Bread, Bread by Ann Morris (HarperTrophy, 1993)

Builder for a Day (DK Children, 2003)

Bunny Cakes by Rosemary Wells (Puffin, 2000)

The Cat Who Came for Tacos by Diana Star Helmer (Albert Whitman and Co., 2003)

Clifford the Big Red Dog by Norman Bridwell (Cartwheel, 1995)

The Coin Counting Book by Rozanne Lanczak Williams (Charlesbridge, 2001)

Corduroy Goes to the Doctor by Don Freeman (Viking Juvenile, 1987)

Curious George and the Puppies by H. A. Rey (Houghton Mifflin, 1998)

Curious George Goes to a Movie by H. A. Rey (Houghton Mifflin, 1998)

Curious George Plays Baseball by Margret Rey (Houghton Mifflin, 1986)

Daddy and Me by Karen Katz (Little Simon, 2003)

A Day in the Life of a Doctor by Linda Hayward (DK Children, 2001)

A Day with a Mail Carrier by Jan Kottke (Children's Press, 2000)

Dear Mr. Blueberry by Simon James (Aladdin, 1996)

Dear Mrs. LaRue: Letters from Obedience School by Mark Teague (Scholastic Press, 2002)

Dear Peter Rabbit by Alma Flor Ada (Aladdin Paperbacks, 1997)

Dinner at the Panda Palace by Stephanie Calmenson (HarperTrophy, 1995)

Doctor Maisy by Lucy Cousins (Candlewick Press, 2001)

Doctor Tools by Inez Snyder (Children's Press, 2002)

Don't Forget the Bacon! by Pat Hutchins (Gardners Books, 2001)

The Donut Book by Sally Levitt Steinberg (Storey Publishing, 2004)

Ella Takes the Cake by Carmela D'Amico (Arthur A. Levine Books, 2005)

A Fish Out of Water by Helen Palmer (Random House Books for Young Readers, 1961)

The Flower Alphabet Book by Jerry Pallotta (Charlesbridge, 1988)

Flower Garden by Eve Bunting (Voyager Books, 2000)

Follow the Money by Loreen Leedy (Holiday House, 2003)

Fox in Socks by Dr. Seuss (Random House Books for Young Readers, 1965)

Fran's Flower by Lisa Bruce (HarperCollins, 2000)

Friday Night at Hodges' Café by Tim Egan (Houghton Mifflin, 1996)

Froggy Eats Out by Jonathan London (Viking Juvenile, 2001)

Froggy Goes to the Doctor by Jonathan London (Viking Children's Books, 2002)

Froggy Plays Soccer by Jonathan London (Puffin, 2001)

Glasses for D. W. by Marc Brown (Random House Books for Young Readers, 1996)

Glasses (Who Needs 'Em?) by Lane Smith (Puffin, 1995)

Grocery Store by Angela Leeper (Heinemann, 2004)

Have You Seen My Cat? by Eric Carle (Aladdin, 1997)

Homer Price by Robert McCloskey (Puffin, 1976)

How Big Is a Foot? by Rolf Myller (Yearling Books, 1991)

I Love My Hair by Natasha Anastasia Tarpley (Megan Tingley, 1998)

I Need Glasses: My Visit to the Optometrist by Virginia Dooley (Mondo Publishing, 2002)

If You Take a Mouse to the Movies by Laura Numeroff (Laura Geringer, 2000)

The Jolly Postman by Janet and Allan Ahlberg (Little, Brown and Co., 2001)

Just a Piggy Bank by Gina and Mercer Mayer (Golden Books, 2001)

Kite Flying by Grace Lin (Dragonfly Books, 2004)

Let's Make Pizza by Mary Hill (Children's Press, 2002)

Little Nino's Pizzeria by Karen Barbour (Voyager Books, 1990)

The Little Red Hen Makes a Pizza by Amy Walrod (Puffin Books, 2002)

Luna and the Big Blur: A Story for Children Who Wear Glasses by Shirley Day (Magination Press, 2000)

Magenta Gets Glasses by Deborah Reber (Simon Spotlight/Nickelodeon, 2002)

The Magic School Bus Gets Baked in a Cake: A Book about Kitchen Chemistry by Joanna Cole (Scholastic, 1995)

Makeup Mess by Robert Munsch (Cartwheel, 2002)

Miss Piggy's Night Out by Sarah Hoagland Hunter (Puffin Books, 1995)

Mmm, Cookies! by Robert Munsch (Cartwheel, 2002)

Mr. Betts and Mr. Potts by Rod Hull (Barefoot Books, 2000)

My Basketball Book by Gail Gibbons (HarperCollins, 2000)

My Football Book by Gail Gibbons (HarperCollins, 2000)

My Soccer Book by Gail Gibbons (HarperCollins, 2000)

NFL: Big and Small (DK Publishing, Inc., 1999)

NFL: Colors (DK Publishing, Inc., 2000)

Nappy Hair by Carolivia Herron (Dragonfly Books, 1998)

Old MacDonald Had a Woodshop by Lisa Shulman (Putnam Juvenile, 2002)

One Bean by Anne Rockwell (Walker Books for Young Readers, 1999)

A Pair of Red Clogs by Masako Matsuno (Purple House Press, 2002)

Pete's a Pizza by William Steig (HarperCollins, 1998)

Pick a Pet by Shelley Rotner (Scholastic, 1999)

Pizza Pat by Rita Golden Gelman (Random House Books for Young Readers, 1999)

The Pizza That We Made by Joan Holub (Puffin Books, 2001)

Planting a Rainbow by Lois Ehlert (Voyager Books, 1992)

     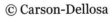

The Popcorn Book by Tomie DePaola (Holiday House, 1984)

The Post Office Book: Mail and How It Moves by Gail Gibbons (HarperTrophy, 1986)

Puppy Mudge Takes a Bath by Cynthia Rylant (Aladdin, 2004)

Rapunzel by Paul O. Zelinsky (Dutton Books, 1997)

Red Lace, Yellow Lace: Learn to Tie Your Shoe by Mark Casey and Judith Herbst (Barron's Educational Series, 1996)

Sally Goes to the Vet by Stephen Huneck (Harry N. Abrams, Inc., 2004)

Shoes by Elizabeth Winthrop (HarperFestival, 1996)

Shoes, Shoes, Shoes by Ann Morris (HarperTrophy, 1998)

Signs at the Store by Mary Hill (Children's Press, 2003)

Smart About Money: A Rich History by Jon Anderson (Grosset and Dunlap, 2003)

Smelly Socks by Robert Munsch (Cartwheel, 2005)

Something Good by Robert Munsch (Annick Press, 1990)

Stephanie's Ponytail by Robert Munsch (Annick Press, 1996)

Sunflower House by Eve Bunting (Voyager Books, 1999)

Things That Are the Most in the World by Judi Barrett (Aladdin, 2001)

This Is Baseball by Margaret Blackstone (Henry Holt and Company, 1997)

This Is the Sunflower by Lola M. Schaefer (Greenwillow Books, 2000)

Tie Your Shoes: Rocket Style/Bunny Ears by Leslie Bockol (Innovative Kids, 2003)

The Tiny Seed by Eric Carle (Aladdin, 2001)

To the Post Office with Mama by Sue Farrell (Annick Press, 1994)

Veggies on Our Pizza by Chantelle B. Goodman (Pentland Press, 2002)

A Visit to the Supermarket by B. A. Hoena (Pebble Plus, 2004)

Walter the Baker by Eric Carle (Aladdin, 1998)

What Do You Want on Your Pizza? by William Boniface (Price Stern Sloan, Inc., 2000)

Where Are You? by Francesca Simon (Peachtree Publishers, 1998)

Who's at the Movies? by Yukiko Kido (Sterling Press, 2006)

Who's Peeking at You? In the Pet Store by Richard Powell (Barron's Educational Series, 2006)

Will Goes to the Post Office by Olof and Lena Landstrom (R and S Books, 2001)

Z is for Zamboni: A Hockey Alphabet by Matt Napier (Sleeping Bear Press, 2002)